HE STILL SPEAKS TODAY

*Releasing the
Dynamic Power
of God's Word
in Your
Life*

JOHN SHERRILL

PUBLISHING
A Ministry Of Youth With A Mission
P.O. BOX 55787, SEATTLE, WA 98155

YWAM Publishing is the publishing ministry of Youth With A Mission. Youth With A Mission (YWAM) is an international missionary organization of Christians from many denominations dedicated to presenting Jesus Christ to this generation. To this end, YWAM has focused its efforts in three main areas:
1) Training and equipping believers for their part in fulfilling the Great Commission (Matthew 28:19). 2) Personal evangelism. 3) Mercy ministry (medical and relief work).
For a free catalog of books and materials write or call:
YWAM Publishing
P.O. Box 55787, Seattle, WA 98155
(206)771-1153 or (800) 922-2143
e-mail address: 75701.2772 @ compuserve.com

He Still Speaks Today
Copyright © 1997 John Sherrill

Published by Youth With A Mission Publishing
P.O. Box 55787
Seattle, WA 98155

ISBN 0-927545-48-9

Printed in the United States of America.

Contents

Introduction to Abridged Version

It has been a privilege to prepare this abridged version of *My Friend the Bible* for publication, and I am indebted to the Lord for the experience. Poring over the manuscript day after day exposed me to much wisdom learned from John Sherrill's walk with God. Of the many spiritual principles this book presents, I would like to draw your attention to three I found particularly helpful:

First, the book urges us to expect the written Word of God to speak to us *personally*. Not that John anticipated that when he first turned to the Bible. But after a while he learned not to be surprised when something within its pages—a phrase, a command or an illustration—gripped his heart, giving him sudden wisdom about an aspect of modern living. It was the solution to a problem, or the inspiration for a course of action to be taken. We live in a day when we need that to happen to more of us. God wants to encourage us, challenge us, guide us or give us correction through His Word.

Second, John Sherrill encourages us to commit to memory those scriptural phrases that will help us resist the pestering power of temptation. His experiences learning to overcome carnal habits—through speaking out phrases from the Bible—is an inspiration to us all.

Third, when we overcome these temptations we can expect a surge of spiritual anointing to follow. This in itself gives added impetus to resist the power of evil.

John has allowed me to write questions on each chapter, and these are found in Appendix Three. I do trust the extra thinking required will add to your spiritual edification and enjoyment. Even if you're not reading this in a school or group context, may I encourage you to take a peek at those questions after you've read a chapter? I believe if you could, it would help you retain more from this gem of a book and thus propel you closer to the Lord whom we all wish to please.

Ross Tooley
University of the Nations
Kona, Hawaii

1

The Old Man's Promise

I felt vaguely uneasy that Sunday morning several years ago as I looked around the bare, echoing room where my hostess was arranging child-sized chairs in a semicircle around her desk. I was visiting friends in a west Texas town. My hostess had asked me to attend the Bible class which she was teaching, and even before the class began I suspected that these men and women were going to know a lot more about Scripture than I did.

As we had come into church a few moments earlier it seemed that every single person was carrying a Bible. It's just a cultural phenomenon, I said to myself. Back home in New York, in our own Episcopal church, if you brought a Bible with you on Sunday it meant you'd been asked to read the Epistle during the communion service. But this was not an Episcopal church in New York, this was a Baptist church in west Texas. And there were Bibles everywhere.

The classroom began to fill up. It was an old man who finally noticed that I was not carrying a Bible. I remember that he had a freshly scrubbed and sunbaked face, and that he carried *two* Bibles. He put them down on a miniature chair, took his coat off, hung it carefully on a wall peg, and sat down. Then he spoke to me.

"Here, young fellow," he said, handing me one of his Bibles. I was gratified that someone could still call me *young* since I was well past forty at the time of that Texas visit, and what was left of my hair was already beginning to gray.

The old man couldn't let me have his *real* Bible, the large, black, leather-bound and dog-eared one. But he did hand me *The Living Bible,* and I felt grateful. Not only for the loan, but because he had given me this particular version: I was one of those people who, in spite of the fact that I had been a Christian for several years, had read the Bible through eagerly shortly after my conversion, and had been an editor on an inter-faith magazine for years, still did not feel really comfortable with the Scriptures. I couldn't seem to get a handle on the book. *The Living Bible,* though, in its green binding, seemed enough like any other book to put me at ease.

My hostess was handing out mimeographed sheets. When mine reached me I noticed with a shudder that it contained a list of Bible references. As surely as I sat in that kindergarten chair I knew we would shortly be going around the circle, looking up passages and reading them aloud.

My eyes scanned the list. I wouldn't have trouble with Genesis, Exodus, Leviticus, Psalms, the Gospels or some of the Letters. But there were those other names on the list, the ones I could never find. Did Habakkuk come before or after Haggai? And for that matter, where was Haggai?

And then, sure enough, my hostess began at the far right. "Charles, would you please read our Philemon?"

Charles flipped to Philemon.

Quickly, I counted the number of chairs between me and Mr. Philemon, and found that I was Second Samuel. Not bad. I riffled the pages of *The Living Bible* and found Second Samuel.

By now it was the next person's turn: she had an easy reference in Acts.

But to my horror my hostess asked Mrs. Acts to read another passage too, which threw my count off. I was no longer Second Samuel. If my count were not thrown off again, I would be Titus. But if one other person should read two passages, I would be— Habakkuk!

I was hoping against hope that the Lord was not in a playful mood, when an out occurred to me. Maybe this Bible had an index! While everyone was paying attention to Mr. Lamentations, I turned to the front of my *Living Bible* and sure enough, there was an index. Surreptitiously I held the book open to that page and waited. Mr. Lamentations finished. Mrs. Ezekiel read a short passage and then, as I had feared, another. I was next—I was Habakkuk! Even as my hostess was saying, "John, would you read the next passage?" my eyes were scanning the index. Sure enough, there it was. Page 715. With the smugness of a schoolboy who has been asked the one question he knows how to answer, I turned *right* to Habakkuk and started reading.

Just as I finished, a merciful bell rang and the class was over.

Then, the first of two fragile events occurred, events which were separated by a few weeks of time but which were prophetic for me in the sense that in them I heard God speaking.

The first of these two events was a statement from the lips of the old man who had lent me his Bible. When it came time for me to give the Bible back to him, he asked the usual polite question, "You here for long, fellow?"

But then, without transition, the old man with the shining chin added the words which I now know came straight from God. He stroked his Bible and said, "This is where you find the answers to your problems."

That was all. The old man turned away.

That afternoon as I was packing for the trip home I came across my own Bible. I took it out of my briefcase and in my mind compared its crisp pages with the much-fingered Bible the old man had brought with him. Why wasn't I using my Bible the way these people were? *This is where you find the answers to your problems* the old man had said. Was I missing something vital? Had these people discovered in their Bibles a quality I never dreamed of? In spite of that first eager reading after my conversion, the Bible remained for me a formidable book, the province of scholars and preachers and grandmothers, a book about God and about people who lived thousands of years ago. It just didn't occur to me that this was also a book about me.

It wasn't until another day, weeks later, that God spoke to me again about my relationship to the Bible.

And as so often happens, He spoke through the casual remark of a friend.

Several years ago I had a second bout with cancer. Out of that fear-filled experience had come a direct, personal encounter with Jesus in a hospital room in New York. With it came a healing, and later a stunning, second personal encounter with the Holy Spirit, all of which I've described in an earlier book.

And that's where the trouble began, because a book that is even partially autobiographical always captures its author at a point in time. A person frozen on the pages of a book is different from the person who goes on living, changing, sometimes growing, sometimes regressing. People who met me in the pages of that book were meeting the me of that era. Those first days after my conversion had been utterly joyful and strangely problem-free. But as time passed I began to recognize the shadow of old habit patterns. The sequence had a familiar ring because I had lived through it in my marriage to Tib. During the first blush of our love affair, our joy in finding each other was so great that we just didn't have time for problems. But the honeymoon wasn't the marriage. Nor was the ecstatic honeymoon experience of conversion what life with Jesus was all about. Bit by bit the Lord began to bring me down to earth, where real growth in Him must take place.

Oh, I didn't understand at the time that Jesus was involved in this reemergence of problems. Quite the contrary. Jealousy, anger, overindulgence, sex fantasies, fear—if I were the sort of person who had these problems, where was the victory Jesus had won for me! I tried my best to push down these ugly aspects of myself. When they wouldn't stay there, I felt more and more guilty.

It was in the middle of this drift into guilty living that I found myself in west Texas, hearing an old man say that the Bible held the answer to our problems.

Just a few weeks later (because I am spiritually deaf and need to be shouted at), the Lord spoke to me a second time about the Bible.

Guideposts magazine, where Tib and I worked, was holding a writer's workshop in Holland. Between classes Tib and I sampled Dutch life. Ignoring the care she usually puts into her trim figure, Tib joined me in Holland's famous chocolate and pastry. Then, in reaction, we switched to raw herring and bicycling for miles along the canals. The little hotel where we were staying was all tile and thatched roof. Our room was on the third floor, which you achieved by way of a series of ladders—the Dutch called them stairs.

Late one night after Tib had gone to bed, I sat up talking with an old friend who was also one of the workshop teachers, Jamie Buckingham.

"I've been meaning to ask you, John," Jamie said, leaning back in his chair and crossing his hands behind his head, "how is your spiritual health?"

"Spiritual health?"

"Yes. You were talking at the workshop today about building scenes. Let's do just that. Here you are in Holland where you and Tib wrote *God's Smuggler*. Let's imagine that Brother Andrew has just driven up to this hotel from another of his Bible smuggling trips behind the Curtain. He hops out of his van and throws his arms around you, Dutch style, and starts to tell you about a narrow escape he had at a border search. He's having a praise service tonight to thank God for his safe return and he wants you to come. Now here comes the tension you're always telling writers to look for, because on this same evening you *also* have a chance to spend time with some old buddies. Which would you prefer?"

Silence.

"Maybe that's unfair. I know you don't care much for meetings. Let's try another scene. You're at home now. It's Sunday, and church time rolls around. Would you rather watch a ball game on TV? Or, you and Tib have to make a decision. Is your first impulse to talk the issues through, or pray them through? In other words, what's your spiritual condition?"

I had to admit the truth. Jamie was sensing something. My spiritual health was shaky and getting worse. I guess it showed. I never had been much of an actor.

So that night, into the small hours, Jamie and I talked about the ebb and flow of spiritual vitality. Jamie called this time the beginning of my Walk in the Spirit. The Leap, he said, launched us into the Christian dimension. The Walk was for life. It was on The Walk that each of us came to grips with his own nature.

Then, just as he was yawning and standing up to leave, Jamie asked *that* question.

He asked it casually, "How close are you staying to the word, John?"

"Do you mean the Bible? Well…I hear Scripture read each Sunday."

"That's a start. But do you read the Bible every day, by yourself?"

"No."

"Then start at once, John. Did you know that most vitamins have to be replenished daily? So does rest. So does muscle tone; your muscles start to deteriorate in three days without exercise.

"Your spirit's health follows the same law. If you don't stay close to the Bible, you'll get spiritually flabby within three days. Then if a problem crops up, you'll have no spiritual power to meet it with."

Jamie left, but I was thinking hard. Twice now I had heard the Lord speak about the Bible. Twice He linked His book to the problems I was facing.

⚊⚊ ⚊⚊

I found that I could not forget that visit to Texas, or that midnight scene in a small Dutch hotel. It was as if the Lord was saying; "The time is here for a new kind of relationship between you and Me. Roll up your sleeves and get to work." He seemed to be urging me to begin by developing a new way of reading the Bible—not the breathless, can't-lay-it-down experience I had known before—but a more disciplined, day-in, day-out approach.

All right. I would try it.

Being book-oriented, I searched the library, went through the volumes on our church's shelves and asked around for good beginner's books about the Bible. There were many such books, and interesting ones too. But I could not find a single one that talked about the relationship between the Bible and the problems that had reasserted themselves into my life.

It looked as if I'd just have to plunge in, study the Bible itself, and see what happened.

2

False Starts

As the weeks passed Tib became worried about me. I could tell because she did *not* ask me to get all those books off the dining room table. If I were going to draw closer to the Bible, as Jamie advised, I was going to do it better than anyone.

Spread all over the room where we ordinarily eat were piles of books, loose-leaf binders and rows of freshly sharpened pencils. There was not only a *Cruden's Concordance,* which listed thousands of Bible verses by their key words, but also the much thicker *Strong's Concordance.*

The pile of books on the dining room table grew. There were Bible dictionaries, books that studied the Scriptures by theme, others that dissected the Bible by tracing its ancient manuscripts.

About this time I was given an assignment by my editor at *Guideposts.* Seeing volumes of his *Interpreter's Bible* disappear every time I came into the office in New York (Tib and I work at our home in the suburbs), Len LeSourd said to me one morning, "You seem to be unusually interested in the Bible these days, John. How about doing a Spiritual Workshop?"

Spiritual Workshops were our teaching feature in the magazine. I leaned back and stared thoughtfully out the grimy window at the New York garment district below and made a suggestion.

Len assigned me a theme on humility and I went to work. Ten days later I had finished a document I was really pleased with. It was, in fact, quite probably the best piece of writing I had done for the magazine. The Workshop included quotes not only from the Bible but from giants like Tillich and Niebuhr and Barth. Tib and I always examine each other's material before turning it in. Usually Tib will have her comments back within the day. This time there was a strange silence. Finally I came right out and asked her, "Well?"

She didn't need to ask what the "Well?" went with. Her rich sense of humor broke forth in her laughing response: "Twenty-three footnotes, dear? For *Guideposts?*"

I phoned Len to say that I was shelving the article for a month.

There seemed to be a peculiar truth about my Biblical research though. I had to put it to use, one way or another. At the next meeting of the prayer group Tib and I go to on Wednesday nights, I found myself, with a modest clearing of the throat, offering to "do a little teaching." Of course there wasn't much anyone could say, so I launched into a discussion of the Spirit's gift of humility, as it is found in the Bible. Halfway through my presentation one of the women in the group interrupted. She had had a recent experience with lack of humility which she wanted to share. I resisted the interruption. The Bible study was my province, and I resented her invasion of my territory. I kept steering the discussion back to the course I had charted, until one of the men laughed out loud: "John, your ego is showing."

That was all, but I heard the message. I wasn't showing the very humility I was so keen to describe.

I can't speak for anyone else, but at least for myself I found a double danger in trying to draw closer to the Bible by starting my own private seminary. As important as scholarship is, I should leave that emphasis alone for now. First, it tended to make me proud, as my friends swiftly pointed out to me. And second, the part of my makeup that needed building up right now was not so much my mind as my spirit. Scholarship put an emphasis on mind. Probably, one day, I would come back to Biblical analysis but it hardly seemed the place to start.

The next day I took *Clarke, Cruden, Strong*, the Bible dictionaries and the rest of the weighty books off the dinning room table. Some I returned to *Guideposts*. Others I put back on their shelves in my own library. Although I still use these books for reference and occasionally read Clarke just for fun, the effort to become a professor was over.

It was eleven o'clock on a summer's workday and I was still sitting in my favorite corner on the side porch, reading. The Bible. This time I wasn't studying about the Bible, I was studying the Bible, and although I sensed that this was a step in the right direction there was, nevertheless, something still out of kilter.

What a difference between the way I read the Bible now and the way I read it just after my conversion. The book was still fascinating, but it had lost a lot of the newness and the reading, to be honest, had a forced quality about it. I'd get up at six and make coffee, thinking about people I knew, like David Wilkerson and Olivia Henry, who spent two, three, four hours a day "in the word." Well, if that was the way Bible reading was done, I'd do even better. I read and made notes, and smiled benignly on Tib when she came down at a reasonable hour to find the coffee already thick with age.

Of course, getting started with my work three hours late put a crimp on the day, but I figured that was the price Bible readers often paid. Working at home has advantages for Tib and me. If I start at seven in the morning or at eleven, nothing but a little knot in my stomach knows the difference.

Or perhaps that's not exactly so. I remember my secretary waiting, evening after evening, while I tried to dash through correspondence I hadn't gotten to during the day. I remember a *Guideposts* rewrite I didn't finish in time to make the issue because I'd been spending mornings with the Bible.

Bit by bit it began to occur to me that I was repeating the same error I had made with my effort at scholarship.

In both cases I was being competitive.

That is, I was comparing myself with others. I was trying to read the Bible *the way I saw other people reading the Bible*. I would be a better Bible scholar than anyone, or I would "stay in the word" longer than anyone. And if this created problems in my work, God would understand even if my boss didn't.

At last I saw clearly that when I spent too many hours reading the Bible I couldn't do my job right. And that was cheating.

I was still determined not to drop my project just because I had made mistakes. One morning I decided that perhaps it would be a good idea to do something I should have done all along—pray.

"Lord," I said, "I'm trying to learn how to read the Bible. I'm not getting very far and I really need Your help."

It was while I was still praying that the insight came. Pride was the problem: it was pride that made me want to compete. "All right, Father. Please accept this as my Prayer of Yielded Pride. Help me to get my ego out of the way so that I can read the Bible as You direct me."

The early-morning sun flooded our porch and peace settled over me such as I had not felt since I began this adventure. My own individual way of reading the Bible may or may not be different from other people's. The important element was to get competitiveness out of the way so that I could find the pattern that was right for me.

Ironically, the route out of competitiveness in Bible reading—for me—was to follow a pre-planned program used by thousands of other people.

The idea occurred to me one day when I was in the Washington Cathedral bookstore and saw a copy of the *Episcopal Church Lectionary*, published each year by Morehouse-Barlow.* I picked it up and immediately knew I had found my answer. For every day in the year, Bible references were given. Each morning and each

---

* See Appendix Two for other pre-selected reading programs.

evening there was a psalm, an Old Testament reading and a New Testament reading—and of reasonable length.

So I bought the lectionary and took it home. Right from the start I was glad I had made this choice. I liked to think that each morning as I read a particular selection, our rector at St. Mark's was reading the same verse, and so were thousands of other Christians across the country.

The lectionary, I soon discovered, had other advantages. It was designed to follow the unfolding Christian story through its main elements, always complete within one year. Each season had a special emphasis. Advent dealt with our need for repentance, Easter with victory, Trinity with service to others, and so on. So the lectionary gave a safe balance to reading: there was less chance of singling out pet passages and ignoring others.

Interesting how Tib, who had shown vast unenthusiasm for my efforts at scholarship and marathon reading, now seemed intrigued by what I was doing. Tib is a history buff; she especially valued the ancient roots of the lectionary system with its origins in Judaism. The Jews of Jesus' day also followed appointed reading in their synagogues. One day she said, "What if I joined you? That way we'd be reading the same passages each day!"

And this was how I stumbled upon the second secret of sustained, personal Bible reading. The first secret was to squelch the longer-than-thou syndrome by reading pre-set selections. The second was to make a pact with someone to read the same passages each day. My pact was with my wife, but it could equally well have been with one of our children, or with someone in our prayer group or our church. Often Tib and I do not read the passages aloud, or even at the same time. But that's unimportant. What is important, we found, was the shared commitment.

I had barely got underway with my new approach to the Bible, however, before an unexpected difficulty began to emerge. I was carrying around inside me, I discovered, other people's feelings about the Bible. These feelings were still powerful. Although in many cases I had not seen the individuals since childhood...

3

The Trap of
Inherited Emotions

I had no idea that I was carrying around a highly charged set of attitudes toward the Bible, picked up from other people. The greatest enemy of intellectual honesty is the opinion of people we value and respect. The people who fell into this category for me impressed their views on my mind with almost indelible force.

One morning when Tib and I sat down in our now cleared dining room to read the Bible together, the first selection from the lectionary was Psalm 18. I began calmly enough.

> *The Lord also thundered in the heavens,*
> *and the Most High uttered his voice,*
> *hailstones and coals of fire.*
> *And he sent out his arrows, and scattered them;*
> *he flashed forth lightnings, and routed them.*
> *Psalm 18:13,14* RSV

Suddenly my heart started to race, my stomach knotted. I put the Bible face up on the table beside me.

"What in the world's the matter?" Tib asked.

"I don't know. It's something in this reading."

Tib picked up the Bible and glanced down the verses. "I don't understand. This psalm is telling about how Jehovah comes to our rescue in times of trouble. It's a poem full of images." She picked up the selection:

> *He bowed the heavens, and came down;*
> *thick darkness was under his feet.*
> *He rode on a cherub, and flew;*
> *he came swiftly upon the wings of the wind.*
> *Psalm 18:9,10* RSV

But all the while Tib was reading I kept having that same half-panicky reaction. Afterwards, our seventeen-year-old, Liz, came down for breakfast before catching the high school bus, and we did not get back to the subject.

Later that day, however, I forced myself to face what had happened. The fact was that those verses had left me upset. They brought back frightening half-forgotten memories. Memories of times when my father, usually the personification of calm, became agitated enough that my small-boy antenna picked up danger signals.

There was one man who came around often to the Presbyterian Theological Seminary in Louisville, Kentucky, where my father was a professor, whose name I never knew. Dad always spoke of the man simply as *him.* And he always spoke with emotion.

"You just can't reason with *him*, Helen." This, in a whispered aside to Mother.

"It's him again!" This, when Dad thought I was out of earshot. "Trying to divide the faculty."

Dad never discussed this squabble with me, but by the time I was ten I had picked up the main outlines. The emotion was attached to the question, "How much of the Bible do you understand as literal, and how much as figurative?" *Him* and his school fought to hold the line against the school, represented by my father, which sought to place the Bible in an historical and literary framework. The Bible, according to *him*, was literally true in every detail, and anyone who thought otherwise was going straight to hell. If the Bible said God rode a cherub, then that is precisely what happened, and to read Scripture in any other way was to undermine the very foundations of Christian faith.

I wonder what Dad would say today if he was alive and knew that I, his own son, was far closer to the position of the literalists than I was to his own. I wonder how we would go about communicating on this subject because it's surprising how incapable Dad was of listening to anything this one man, *him*, had to say. That wasn't like Dad. People from all over the country came to our red brick house in the Highlands of Louisville to seek Dad's help with anguishing, personal problems. They came because he was open-hearted and knew how to listen. Yet with *him*, Dad never really tried.

The war spread. One winter day I happened to be with Dad in the living room as he was going through his mail.

"Not again!" he exploded, and then the words slipped out, "I'll bet *he's* behind this." I looked at the envelope Dad was holding. The letter wasn't from *him*, because *he* was an educated man and this envelope had been addressed in a penciled scrawl. Dad ripped it open, glanced at it hurriedly, then threw both letter and envelope into the wastebasket.

I wanted to learn more.

"Who was that from?" I asked.

"A man who wants to fight with me," Dad said.

"No really, who is it from, Dad?" I fished the letter out of the wastebasket and just had time to notice that the penciled return address was from a small town in the mountains of Kentucky.

"It's not important," my father said, taking the letter back and throwing it, this time, into the fire. "The man is threatening me. Let's go see if lunch is ready."

I didn't enjoy that lunchtime, wondering if the man would come and if he would shoot Mother and my sister Mary and me as well.

So I learned about this controversy in a quite personal way. Men of liberal thought were asking questions. How did science mesh with the truth revealed in the Bible? How did modern psychological insights fit the Biblical viewpoint? Dad was one of the early pioneers in the now widely accepted discipline of pastoral counseling. And the truth he perceived did seem to bear fruit. Dad's own caring insights brought wholeness to young pastors. He could relate the story of Jesus' healing the withered hand so inspiringly that men were, in fact, transformed.

As a boy I observed all this, and I was impressed. Heroes and villains were clearly outlined. Heroes were people who tried to be honest in their thinking, even though it shattered taboos. Villains—at the time, it never even occurred to me to think otherwise—were those who held to the literal interpretation of the Bible.

In time I too came in for hostility. I remember once in my early teens going with my father and mother to a fashionable white-pillared home in a well-to-do section of Louisville. It was a small gathering, half a dozen families, and it soon became clear that one particular guest, a lanky Scotsman with heavy, bright red eyebrows, was keeping a weather eye on me. I even wondered if this man were *him*, and he may indeed have been, for half way through the party he cornered me on the sunporch and made me sit down. I remember how his red eyebrows bobbed up and down as he commanded me to pay attention. He was going to straighten me out on the Bible, this same Bible which he held in his hand. If my eyes wandered, the Scotsman would reach over and grasp my chin and twist my face around so that I was forced to look at him. "Listen to me, John. It says right here that the flood covered the whole earth. That means all of it, every continent, every mountain top."

People who believed the Bible, it seemed, weren't even kind. People who respected the Bible but didn't *believe* much of it were considerate. Maybe they didn't find much mystic support from Scripture but they believed man should be strong in the face of his troubles.

Dad was. A few years after my encounter with the Scot of the flaming eyebrows, while I was in basic training in the Army, Dad went almost totally blind. All he had left was a little peripheral vision that let him walk around his classroom or apartment. He went right on with his teaching and writing schedule, reading more (through Braille and Talking Books) than I did.

After he lost his eyesight, Dad was called to Union Theological Seminary in New York. The only dishonesty I ever caught him at was an odd one. Dad thought blindness was disconcerting to people, distracting them from what he was saying. So he carried notes to his lectern in class, or turned pages of the Bible in the pulpit at the Union chapel, pretending to read but in fact reciting by heart passages locked in his phenomenal memory. Once, years later, I met a man who had been a student under Dad at Union. He heatedly refused to believe that my father had been unable to see.

So, as I say, I had a real hero to look up to and admire in Dad, and some pretty unpleasant people in *him* and his ilk. And my considered view of the matter received still further support.

I'll never forget, as a new reporter for *Guideposts,* being sent by the magazine to interview a trapeze artist who was also an evangelist. I caught up with the aerialist in a little church in Vermont where he was holding services.

It happened, the week before the revival, that there had been a collision outside of town between a gasoline truck and a private automobile. In the fire that followed the car's two passengers were burned to death. The night I was there, with a kind of sick glee the trapeze artist described the deaths in crackling detail, then compared that fearful event to the unquenchable fires of hell that we would all most certainly experience if we did not come forward then and there in answer to his altar call.

So I was pretty well conditioned to react negatively to the subject of Biblical literalness.

And I don't think I am alone in having these visceral emotions. Most of us, approaching the Bible, bring to it a set of preconceived notions and subconscious assumptions which we have inherited from our past. Some of us grew up feeling that the Bible is not important one way or another; it is simply another ancient book. Others unconsciously disparage it, putting it down as the province of ignorant people. Still others may bring to the Bible an almost idolatrous attitude, like a friend of ours who will never place another book, or even a pencil, on top of it, a carryover from the days when few people could read, and the Bible was processed through the church as an object of worship.

The point is that just about everyone carries around attitudes toward the Bible which predate his actual experience with it. In my own case, I had a lot of groundwork to do before I could examine the question of Biblical literalness. I had to identify the childhood emotions I was bringing to the subject and then, to the best of my ability, suspend those reactions and start afresh, letting the Bible speak to *me*.

And in the meanwhile some very different experiences had to be woven into my understanding of the world around me.

The first experience was the physical healing to which I referred at the opening of this story. How fresh the scene remains for me. There I was, kneeling with Tib before the little altar in our home-town church in Mt. Kisco, New York, shortly after I'd been told my cancer had returned. There was our parish priest, Marc Hall, standing behind us. Now he was laying his huge hands on my head. I was numbed, afraid. But suddenly something happened which broke through this dullness. Marc's hands had barely touched my head when power surged through him, entered my body, burning. The heat localized at the very place where the head-and-neck specialist at New York's Memorial Hospital had identified the return of those damning lumps. We left the church, and checked into the famous cancer hospital. The surgeon operated, just hours after the prayer for healing. He found nothing but dried up nodules.

The second event took place shortly after the first. Now it is late at night. I am in my room at Memorial Hospital just after coming down from Recovery. I am in intense pain, but two other men in the room with me seem to be in still worse condition; one is coughing so desperately that I worry for his life; the other, a youngster, is moaning in agony. Quietly, softly into that dark hospital room comes a light which at first I assume is a light carried by a nurse, so real, so illuminating is it. But the light grows in intensity. In warmth. In...personality. I know Who it is. In the company of that infinite caring the first thing that occurs to me is to ask Jesus to touch my two roommates. Jesus responds. The coughing stills. The moans stop.

The third event took place in an ordinary hotel room in Atlantic City, New Jersey. A few Christians had come here to pray with me to be filled with the Holy Spirit. At first I was self-conscious and resisting. But then…into my mind came the memory of my encounter with light. That night in the hospital, I had been able to concentrate on Jesus only. And so it was now too. Suddenly, from deep within begins a joyous, powerful communication so direct and intimate that I cannot contain it. I hear my own voice speaking a language I never learned.

━━━ ━━━

These three experiences represented something new. My cancer was healed, not figuratively but literally. The light I saw in the hospital room was able to reach out and touch suffering men. Speaking in unlearned languages was an audible phenomenon, not a figurative way of stating that faith can enable man to communicate.

As I cautiously came to grips with the literalness of these events I saw that I had some serious thinking to do.

Maybe Dad was wrong.

Maybe, for instance, the man in the synagogue that Sabbath had a physically shriveled up hand, just as the Bible said. It seemed more and more likely that flesh and bone had changed in front of a disbelieving congregation and that from then on the man had a workable hand. From what I had seen in my own life I was ready to believe that this was a literal, precise description of what Jesus did one day.

My understanding was making a huge arc. I started out with an emotional heritage which told me that most of the Bible was allegory. I still did not see *everything* in the Bible as factual description. Some passages are poetic, some are meant to be understood as figure. A good example is in Jesus' statement, "I tell you the truth, no one can see the kingdom of God unless he is born again." Nicodemus tried to take this literally, asking, "How can a man be born when he is old? Surely he cannot enter a second time into his mother's womb to be born!" But Jesus corrected him with some amusement, "You are Israel's teacher, and do you not understand these things?" He then went on to explain the metaphor (John 3:3,4,10 ff.)

With these clear exceptions I was beginning to see larger and larger portions of the Bible as literal events.

But truth dwelt in these accounts at a still deeper level. As I was grasping the huge fact of literalness, I was still only part way into the awesome reality of this Book.

For the truth in the Bible was also contemporary. It had happened then; it was also happening now. Even literalness was not so important as tense.

And even *this* was not the end of the adventure. I had to see these present-tense events as happening *to me. I am* a kind of Abram, setting out from my own familiar homeland, not knowing what lies ahead. I *am* one of the believers gathered in the Upper Room as we are all filled with the Holy Spirit. I *am* a man who has been told he will soon die, a man whom Jesus heals.

What a turnabout. I do wish Dad were alive so we could talk about these things. What would he say if one night we sat quietly by the fire and I finally confided to him how I've come to feel? Could I tell this man how much I love him…but think he is wrong?

4

Facing Problems
in God's Company

*T*en minutes ago Tib and I had landed at LaGuardia Airport where we were met by our son Donn, who had just finished college. Donn took our bags and with his athletic skills showing, dodged New Yorker-style through traffic to the parking lot.

All the while he was talking about how mixed-breed dogs were superior to full-blooded animals.

"For example," Donn said, as he put our suitcases in the trunk, "there's the blend of Husky and German Shepherd. Friend of mine says this is the ideal mix."

On the way to the exit ramp: "A man ought to have a dog."

At the toll gate on the Whitestone Bridge: "A good watchdog is important these days."

A little later at a self-service station, while Donn was filling the tank, Tib took off her glasses and let out a sigh. "Like it or not there's a puppy sitting in our basement this minute."

I stared at her. As our three children one by one left home, the house had taken on a welcome calm. Tib and I could go to bed early, or leave on interview trips with no more forethought than turning the lock on the front door. Suppose Tib was right and Donn did

have a dog in our basement? My mind leaped ahead to the inter-
ference this would bring. The animal would probably bark all
night. I once knew a Husky who bit little children. I'd also known
a Shepherd who went for the throat first and growled later. Besides,
Donn hadn't talked this over with us. He waited until we were away
on a trip...

Donn was replacing the hose. "Do you know for sure?" I whispered quickly to Tib. "That he has a dog, I mean."

"I know Donn for sure. All this propaganda's leading somewhere."

I spent the next twenty miles talking—as if theoretically—
about the impossibility of having a dog, especially a young, noisy
one, with our offices at home, and our trips so frequent. Donn was
silent.

We pulled into our driveway. "Let's go through the basement,"
Donn said heavily.

And there, of course, was the dog.

Donn had rigged up a pen next to my basement office. The
pup's stomach was distended, one ear flopped forward, one back,
his tail whirled. He was visibly untrained.

He didn't look much like a cross between German Shepherd
and Husky, either. I asked Donn about that.

"I told them at the pound..." Donn picked up his dog, "what I
wanted. Just by *coincidence* the man happened to have my dog." Tib
raised her eyes skyward.

For the rest of the day no one brought up the subject of dogs.
But the battle was on nevertheless. I told Donn we were angry
because he had gotten the dog behind our backs. Donn was leaving
home in a couple of months to do graduate work in International
Business Management but until then, he said, this was still his home
and didn't he have a right to have a dog if he wanted one!

So the battle went on. But wouldn't this be a perfect opportunity to probe further the idea of the old man in Texas, that in the
Bible we can find answers to our problems? Could it be that the
Bible spoke to homely, everyday problems such as I was facing with
this odd threat to my peace? I'd find out.

Next morning, awakened early by Donn's dog, I got up, made coffee and went down to my office intending to read the daily lectionary there. But the basement reeked. Annoyance pricked me again. I was all the more aggravated because I had to admit the little animal was friendly! I started to pick up his fouled newspaper but decided against it. No, this was Donn's dog and the mess went with him, too.

Back upstairs, I went into the living room, sat down in my favorite corner of the sofa and opened my Bible to the psalm appointed for that morning. To be honest, I wasn't expecting much to happen. It was the 47th Psalm:

> *Clap your hands, all you nations;*
> *shout to God, with cries of joy.*
> *How awesome is the Lord Most High,*
> *the great King over all the earth!*
> *He subdued nations under us,*
> *peoples under our feet.*
> *He chose our inheritance for us,*
> *the pride of Jacob, whom he loves!*

I was right. Nothing to do with that dog!

> *God has ascended amid shouts of joy,*
> *the Lord amid the sounding of trumpets.*
> *Sing praises to God, sing praises;*
> *sing praises to our King, sing praises.*
> *For God is the King of all the earth;*
> *sing to him a psalm of praise.*
>
> *Psalm 47:1-7* NIV

I put the Bible down abruptly! I couldn't go on. There was something in this second stanza that caught my attention for reasons which I could not understand. That stanza seemed important somehow, as if it were speaking just to this situation. Sing praises…

I sat up straighter. Upstairs I heard someone stirring. Sing praises.

Why did this phrase seem to have a peculiar sticking quality? I was especially puzzled because the very word "praise" had been a problem to me. I knew too many people who abused it, using it on every occasion, often with a peculiar sing-song lilt. "Well pa-raise God!" They used it as a synonym for "thanks." "Praise You, Lord! Thank You, Lord, for letting my son catch pneumonia!" When you are *thankful* to someone for something you imply that he is responsible. And I couldn't understand how God could cause a child to catch pneumonia nor for that matter could I believe that He had put a yelping little creature in my basement.

But the phrase wouldn't let me go. I remembered my friend Bill Henley, a member of our prayer group, once pointing out that praise is trust. That did change the overtone of the word. It shifted the time emphasis from the past to the future. Praise was not so much thanking God for what has happened, as trusting Him for what is going to happen. The element of joy is based on what is to come. "Praise You, Lord. I trust Your love, even though my son has pneumonia."

Was that why I had been stopped? "Are You saying Lord, that You want me to trust You today, even in this annoying situation? I worry about my precious peace instead of trusting You. I'm not counting on You to grant me enough quiet for my work. This is why I got so upset with Donn."

Even as I spoke my heart lifted. I went back to the psalm and read again, rapidly, for I heard footsteps on the stairs. "Sing praises to God…" Trust Him for what's going to happen. "Lord," I said quickly, under my breath, as Donn came into the living room, "I do trust You with this dog. I believe that You can turn it into something wonderful…"

"Morning, Donn," I said aloud. "Sleep well? Your dog will be mighty glad to see you."

I don't want to lean too heavily on one little dog, but it is in these intimate adventures that a lot is revealed. Donn decided to call his dog Lobo, Spanish for *wolf*. That same day while I was practicing trust, Lobo began to show symptoms that were alarming. He was vomiting, and his stomach looked more than usually distended. Donn took his dog to the vet, who insisted on keeping him overnight. Donn returned deflated and reported the vet as saying, "That dog is no mixture of Shepherd and Husky. If I read the signs right, you'll have to change his name from Lobo to Lobito." Lobito means little, very little wolf.

I was making some progress toward appropriating a new attitude about Donn's dog. That night before putting out the light I turned to the evening readings, and as had occurred that morning, a passage seemed to call attention to itself. Again, the portion happened to be from a psalm. The writer recounted all the help God had given Israel, yet the people continually grumbled. They doubted that God could spread a table in the wilderness even though He had just supplied them with water.

> *Therefore, when the Lord heard, he was full of wrath;*
> *a fire was kindled against Jacob,*
> *his anger mounted against Israel;*
> *because they had no faith in God,*
> *and did not trust his saving power.*
> *Psalm 78:21,22* RSV

The message of this strangely highlighted section was extremely clear. I was behaving in the same way that the people of Israel had acted. I was grumbling. I was unhappy with the dog and with Donn because I "had no faith in God, and did not trust his saving power."

That same night I determined by simple willpower not to let this doubting go on. For twenty minutes by the clock I recalled times when God's power had come to help us. I thought of Donn's dog, sitting now in a dark cage at the vet's. I spoke aloud to Tib the first words to come into my mind.

"Do you suppose Lobo's all right?"

Tib looked at me amused. "That dog's getting through to you, isn't he?"

"Something is. That's for sure."

The next morning, early, Donn went down to get his dog. Lobo was all right, thank You, Lord. The vet thought the vomiting stemmed from a poor diet before Lobo came into our household.

Donn put his dog in the pen downstairs. Later that morning I came out of my office and saw Lobito in his usual position, standing on his hind feet, tail whirling.

I reached down and patted him.

Then I found myself picking him up.

Surreptitiously, I took him out to the back yard and let him chase me. Right at the height of the romp I happened to glance toward the dining room window.

There stood Tib and Donn. They were both laughing.

Words That Burn

A strange thing had happened twice in a row. It had been as if the Bible were mysteriously activated, so that a portion was charged with power intended just for my right-now situation.

Something similar to this had happened to the disciples themselves. Discouraged, defeated, lost, they met the resurrected Jesus on the road to Emmaus. He seemed at first to be just another traveler. But then His words began to take a peculiar turn. "Did not our hearts burn within us while he talked to us on the road, while he opened to us the scriptures?" the disciples later asked (Luke 24:32 RSV). It was the same phenomenon I had experienced reading the Bible. My heart burned within me as specific words were illuminated.

Could it be that Jesus is still opening the Scriptures to us? Individually? Now? As we face specific problems?

The question was so vital that I began asking other Christians if they had noticed the same thing and almost without exception they had. People used different words to describe this mysterious activity. Some said words "stopped" them; others said the words made them pay attention or "leaped out of the page"; still others said that words were "spotlighted" or that "they seemed to speak aloud." But always the message was the same: the Bible had a way of talking individually to the reader through words that burned.

As if to encourage me in my discovery, the next week I found these words on the back of a calling card:

"I am sorry for the men who do not read the Bible every day. I wonder why they deprive themselves of the strength and of the pleasure. It is one of the most singular books in the world, for every time you open it, some old text that you have read a score of times suddenly beams with a new meaning. There is no other book that I know of, of which this is true: there is no other book that yields its meaning so personally, that seems to fit itself so intimately to the very spirit that is seeking its guidance."

The words were Woodrow Wilson's.

It is hard to describe the excitement I felt. I had a new reason for reading the Bible. Every day I could bring some real-life situation to the Scriptures. It could be a problem, an intercession, a decision, my own need or someone else's. With this on my mind I would read until Jesus spoke to me through words that glowed.

And so I began a life-changing experiment. One day the beaming verse would speak words of encouragement, another day words of correction. They might bring specific instruction or simply an expression of His love. But the verses always had one thing in common. They were unbelievably on target. They always spoke as a person would speak who knew me thoroughly, who knew what I was facing, who grasped my situation, from the tiniest details to the overall picture, far more clearly in fact than I did myself.

One morning, for instance, I faced an emergency deadline. I had to do three days' worth of work for the magazine in just a few hours, a situation that called for more energy and boldness than I possessed. That day Mark 4:40 (KJV) spoke directly to me. "He said to his disciples, 'Why are you so afraid? Do you still have no faith?'" Every time during that day when my enervating fears rose up, this verse had the power to encourage.

On another day I had just watched a spectacular sunset, only to open the Bible to the appointed readings "The heavens are telling the glory of God; and the firmament proclaims his handiwork" (Psalm 19:1 RSV). Tib began to have the experience too. On the first night of a visit to the whaling center of Nantucket she read;

Yonder is the sea, great and wide,
which teems with things innumerable,
living things both small and great.
There go the ships,
and Leviathan which thou didst form to sport in it.
Psalm 104:25,26 RSV

Sometimes the stopping verse took on a correcting note. One day I was suffering an unusual kind of pain. We were in the middle of a seven-months-long drought in New York. Corn, which should have been "knee high in July," was barely six inches tall. Our lawn had browned out, but watering was forbidden. The creek in our back yard was a trickle. Trees curled their leaves in protest.

Now, I have never understood why water, plenty of water, is so important to me. Tib loves the desert, but I do not. Lack of water causes me personal pain. I try to pull moisture out of the air. I yearn for it, suffer with the ground. It is a visceral experience, beyond logic.

One morning during my living room reading time I was again feeling this pain when suddenly a set of words came into sharper-than-usual focus.

"Offer to God a sacrifice of thanksgiving…" (Psalm 50:14 RSV).

What did that mean? I tried to read on, but the verse pulled me back. I *could* give thanks, of course, right in this drought, as an act of will. But it would indeed be a kind of sacrifice, a costly and diffi-cult thing to do in the midst of the arid reality I saw around me.

"I think I'm hearing You, though," I mused, there at my sofa-corner post in the living room. "I doubt You want me to give thanks for the drought itself, but I can live through my Sahara in an atti-tude of thanksgiving. I give You thanks for the water we do have. Thanks for the abundant crops we usually enjoy. Thanks for the fact that we have plenty of food." The rest of the day whenever dust eddies blew past the window I deliberately put myself into a mood of appreciation and thankfulness, even when a negative mood would have *seemed* appropriate.

It made all the difference. Not just for that day, but for the dura-
tion of the drought. I was able to live through the rest of the almost
rainless summer in an attitude of joy by leaning on this verse from
the Psalms.

So my experiment proceeded. I kept at my reading, confident
that I would receive a special word from the Lord each day.

Then one morning, after I had been at my program for some
weeks, a strange thing happened. No illuminated verse appeared.
The next day was the same. Occasionally, over the following two
weeks, I would be given a highlighted verse, but it lacked force and
immediacy. Which perhaps explains why, when words at last did
make themselves known to me in the familiar, blazing way, I felt a
sense of great excitement.

"If I had cherished iniquity [sin] in my heart, the Lord would
not have listened," said Psalm 66:18 (RSV).

"All right, Lord, there must be something between us. Would
You tell me what it is?"

Almost immediately sprang to mind a still-smarting memory.
Just a couple of weeks before (right at the time I began to have trouble hearing God in the Bible) I had been cheated out of two hundred dollars, a lot of money at the time. Tib and I have long wanted
to own a piece of land on which we might someday build a smaller,
retirement house. I saw an ad in the *New York Times* for several acres
of wild, rocky land that sounded just exactly right, and called the
number. Soon I was tramping over hills, talking about perc tests and
imagining where a house could go.

"I'm trying to settle an estate," the owner told me. "That's why
this price is so low. Are you interested?"

"Definitely. But I want my wife to see it."

"Sorry. Other people are..." He didn't finish his sentence
because an idea occurred to him. "Why don't you just put down a
binder? It doesn't have to be much. Two hundred will do. If you
change your mind I'll give you your money back."

Which I did. Tib came with me the next day to see the property and we both agreed that it was just right. So I called up the owner and told him he had a deal.

"Well…" he said. "You see…"

And I knew there was a problem. The owner had decided not to sell after all. He was sorry. I was disappointed, but I didn't want to hold him to his binder, so the owner agreed to send me a check since he had already cashed my own. Three days passed. A week. No check. I called the owner and received an astonished, "You haven't got your money yet! I'll speak to my secretary. It'll be in the mail today." Nothing. That went on for another week with my phone calls becoming more and more frequent. I asked an attorney what I could do and he assured me that recovery would cost more than what I'd paid out.

So I quit calling, but my emotions were still fighting. In my mind I played and replayed conversations with this man if he ever did call back. Which he didn't.

"Do you know where he lives?" Tib asked when I brought up my dilemma at the supper table. "If he won't return your calls you could go over there."

Which we did, that same night. The owner's house was dark. A neighbor was walking a dog. "They've gone to Florida for the winter," he told us.

I started to back out of the man's driveway, defeated. "You can't just leave, honey," Tib said. "You haven't resolved a thing."

"There's nothing more I can do. Unless maybe we sit here and pray for the guy." I was half joking, but Tib treated the idea seriously. So, there in the owner's driveway, she and I said what was, for us, an unusual prayer. We released the owner from any judgment on our part. We couldn't see him face to face, but we asked the Lord to heal whatever hurt there was in his life that made him act in a way that must be costing him peace and joy too.

Tib turned on the domelight and looked at me closely. "Lord," she added, "You know how upset this has made John. If there is anything left in him of anger, hurt pride, feeling that he should stand up for his rights, we just ask You to take that over too. Do for John what he can't do for himself."

"Amen," I said.

Yet despite that prayer, it was not until I found this "Power Verse" (Ps. 66:18) that the word completed what prayer had started. I completely forgave the man.

And the results? We never did get our money back. But that night the Scriptures opened to me again. "…do not fret when men succeed in their ways, when they carry out their wicked schemes." (Psalm 37:7 NIV). I was accustomed to illuminated readings, but this one was astonishing. It was as if the Lord was saying, "It's good to have your ear again."

So that was the beginning of what was, for me, a new way to read the Bible. I found that illumination could shine on just a few words or on a whole section. The stopping verse could come immediately, or at the end of the reading, or even, indeed, outside the prescribed reading altogether. I learned to put down my Bible for a moment when I got to my verse. I would live with that word, mull it over, listen.

Sometimes the lectionary wasn't involved at all. One day I was in Houston on a story for *Guideposts*. The interview with the astronaut went badly and I knew that I had failed in my assignment. There was no point writing up my slim notes so I was left with a lot of time on my hands, disappointed, far away from home…a bad combination for me.

And to make matters worse I had forgotten to bring my Bible and lectionary. I opened the formica drawer in the formica table in the motel room and there, among the laundry lists and room service cards, was a Gideon Bible. I opened it, flipped idly through the pages, browsing in Isaiah. I began to read the sixty-second chapter. Nothing. I read on, into the next chapter. Nothing.

But then there it was, complete and satisfying, an illuminated single phrase. At first it didn't seem apropos: "In all their affliction he was afflicted…" the passage said (Isaiah 63:9 KJV). But then I understood. The Lord Himself was sharing this disappointment and this boring evening with me. He knew all about the failure, too. He was hurting with me and could empathize.

I picked up the phone and called home to have a long, leisurely talk with Tib. All that evening and all the way back home without my story I felt excited. What a helpful passage! What a useful tool!

5

Two Kinds of Power

*T*wo days later I was thinking again about that experience in Houston. I opened my Bible to the passage I had found and read it over. "In all their affliction he was afflicted..." I expected a return of the excitement I had experienced there in my hotel room, when I had been so frustrated and lonesome and had been strongly supported by the Bible.

Instead, the verse seemed flat.

What was the matter? How could a verse be full of life one day, seemingly empty the next? I went through my Bible to see if this were also true of other passages which seemed so vital when I first read them. Time after time it was true. The Psalm passage that helped me praise God for Lobo—it seemed a bit ordinary now. The reading that lifted "my" sunset into still another realm of glory—when I read it over now, it seemed lackluster. It was almost as if the passages had been infused with unusual life for those special occasions.

Manna Verses

Maybe it was like that hibiscus. Tib's grandparents lived in Miami Beach. Every morning Papa went into his backyard to pick a red hibiscus blossom for Goggie's breakfast table. The first time I saw him do this I was surprised that he simply placed the fragile crepe-like bloom on the table.

"Shouldn't that flower be in water?" I whispered to Tib.

Tib smiled at my northern innocence. "That wouldn't help," she explained. "There's nothing you can do to keep an hibiscus blossom. Whether you leave it on the table or put it in water, it can last for just one day."

And so had that verse I found in the hotel room in Houston. Were highlighted verses often *meant* to last only for a span of time? Perhaps for the space of a particular project, where pinpointed direction or support was especially needed? Perhaps, sometimes, for a week or just a day or even for a few hours. It would make sense. There is a here-then-gone quality about so many valuable things. A smile, a snowflake, a perfect family meal with everyone there. This is often God's way of giving us His favorite gifts too. I re-read Exodus 16, where Moses is explaining manna to Israel. It was the bread which the Lord had given the people to eat, Moses said. But it was a right-now gift:

> *Each morning everyone gathered as much as he needed, and when the sun grew hot, it melted away.*
> Exodus 16:21 KJV

Manna was sufficient, perfect food for a span of time. But if it was kept past that time, then it spoiled (Exodus 16:20) or melted (Exodus 16:21). And so it was with many stopping verses. Later, if I went back over the reading, the once brimming passage just didn't speak in the same way. I could still remember the warmth and security that had come to me, yesterday, when I had been held close by God, but it was just a memory; like a dream, it was almost impossible to recapture the sense of immediacy I had experienced the day before.

Apparently the Lord wanted me to come to Him each day for spiritual fellowship to see me through that day's needs.

I must admit that I had a nag-and-pester worry. It started as a fleeting question, but grew in intensity. Maybe there was nothing truly supernatural in these Manna Verses, nothing unexplainable about what was happening. Perhaps it was just an accident. Could I have found help because I *wanted* to find it, nothing more?

Then, one morning, these words were singled out for me.

> *For we do not have a high priest who is unable to sympa-*
> *thize with our weaknesses, but we have one who has been*
> *tempted in every way, just as we are—yet was without sin.*
> Hebrews 4:15 NIV

What was this verse saying to me! I actually tried to ignore the subtle brightness because it just didn't relate to any problem I could think of; I was not aware of any special temptations at the moment.

Then, in that afternoon's mail came a royalty report. It was clear even at a glance that the publisher had made a mistake in our favor. A decimal place had got in the wrong column and we were being paid ten times the amount we were supposed to receive. Tib and I had unusual dental expenses that month and the larger check would have been welcome indeed.

But the temptation never had a chance, for there was the high-lighted "Manna Verse" from that morning. I repeated it aloud, hearing it tell me that Jesus sympathized with my temptations, that He had been tested too, and yet He had not sinned. With Him as high priest interceding, it was a simple matter—a very simple matter really—to pick up the phone and get the error straightened out.

But wait a minute! As I put the phone back in its cradle, I had a spine-tingling realization. I had not brought this temptation to the Bible and then received a Manna Verse. It was the other way around. Something strictly supernatural had occurred. This Manna Verse was highlighted for me *before* the temptation took place. It couldn't have been me, looking for a helping hand and finding one. The word was given beforehand; then when it was needed, there it was ready to defend me.

An even more unexplainable event occurred a few weeks later. On that morning as I sat reading, a verse again "lit up" that didn't seem to have relevance to my life; perhaps this too was being highlighted for a problem in the future.

"Blessed are they that do his commandments," the verse said, "that they may have right to the tree of life, and may enter in through the gates into the city" (Revelation 22:14 KJV).

I simply could not imagine how that passage would ever be important. I waited all through the afternoon, expectantly. Nothing came up that had any conceivable bearing on the quote.

Suppertime came and I was as puzzled as ever. Tib was out of town and I had a dinner date with a young bachelor who was planning to sell his grocery business and go into full-time work with runaway kids in New York City. My bachelor friend thought the Lord had told him to make the move, yet lately everything had come to a stop. No buyer appeared for his store, the work he had already begun with young people in the city seemed to stagnate. He couldn't tell why.

How can I describe the feeling of awe, as I saw suddenly that the verse I had memorized that morning might fit not my situation, but my friend's? "Blessed are they that do his commandments, that they...may enter into the city." Was he *not* entering his city because he was in some particular *not* doing the Lord's commandments? Yet how dare I bring that up!

We went on eating for ten minutes, with my verse humming in my mind, struggling, I suppose, to be expressed.

Finally I could take it no longer.

"Stan," I said, "are you by any chance disobeying God in some way?"

Stan began to stir his coffee so rapidly that it spilled out over the side of his cup.

I then explained why I was asking that question, quoting to him the verse that had been singled out of my morning-time reading.

Stan stirred his coffee, on and on. Finally, he took the spoon out, flicked off a last drop and leaned back.

"You *couldn't* have known," he said hoarsely.

Then he told me about an affair he was having with a married woman. It was a liaison, he said, that he now knew he would have to break if he ever wanted to enter his city and be effective with young people.

"It's not that I *didn't* know before," he said in a whisper, still awed, "it's that I didn't want to hear. But that verse of yours…" He laughed, not wanting to finish the sentence. And indeed he didn't need to go on. We both had witnessed the Lord in the act of stating how intimately He knows us, how individual is His caring.

Arsenal Verses

Tib and I were in Chicago for book interviews with Demos Shakarian, an Armenian with a dynamic ministry in the United States. Demos is a remarkable man in a great many ways, not the least of which is his energy. He thrives on long conventions and five-hour banquets, *then* wants to start our interviews.

Now Demos was calling to ask if we could meet for some work just after midnight. We agreed, but I knew what would happen. Tib would give out around two, but Demos would want to tell just one more story.

And that's what did happen.

There I was, sleepy and tired, yet anxious because I knew our schedule did not mesh easily with the Shakarians'. While Demos was pouring the last of the coffee from a silver bottle, I found myself wondering if there were any way I could use the Bible in this situation. Unfortunately Demos was now in the middle of the story of a remarkable bull-calf he once bought. It wouldn't do to just stop life and open my Bible, hoping that a Manna Verse would come to my rescue.

In a culture like ours nearly everyone has a few Bible verses in his memory bank. A fragment of the Twenty-third Psalm came to mind: "…he restores my soul…" While Demos was relating his story into the cassette I took advantage of this passage by repeating it a few times to myself under my breath.

And sure enough, a quiet infusion of strength came to me. It was Demos himself who finally looked at his watch and was surprised at the hour. So we said good night and left.

With more than just a series of good notes, too. Because as I was putting on my pajamas by the light that came in from the street, so as not to wake Tib, I suddenly understood the experience I'd just had. I had stumbled onto an entirely *different* way God has of using His word. The verse I used was not a Manna Verse, coming right from the pages of the Bible, oddly fragile, like dew. This verse had been stored in my mind for years, ready, waiting. It seemed as if there were two distinct uses of Scripture; one was a Manna Verse, given by the Bible especially for today; the other was a memorized verse which perhaps could even be used over and over again.

A few days later, on our way home from Chicago, a winter storm forced long delays at O'Hare. At six o'clock in the morning we were sitting on a hard, plastic, vandal-proof bench in the airport waiting room. We were harassed; we were exhausted. It was another situation where we needed a surge of strength. Perhaps the phrase from the Twenty-third Psalm would be helpful a second time? If so, this would be something new, because up until now the verses that were given as manna tended to go flat.

"Honey, do you remember what the Bible promises? 'He restores my soul...' Let's ask the Lord to give us that strength right now."

It was a beautiful thing watching the energy hidden in this word take control of our selves. We relaxed and waited, restored. When we did get on a flight we were refreshed. Even the crusty scrambled eggs served on the airline's best styrofoam seemed flavored with His caring.

⬤ ⬤ ⬤ ⬤

Sometimes, then, God's provision *could* be stored, like weapons in an arsenal. These were valuable weapons, these "Arsenal Verses." Surely I had some more stashed away! I remembered another which ministers were always using at the beginning of services. "I was glad when they said unto me, Let us go into the house of the Lord" (Psalm 122:1 KJV). And there was another which I remembered because it was carved in soot-streaked limestone above the gothic entrance to the seminary where my father taught in Louisville: "Surely I will be with you always" (Matthew 28:20 NIV).

They were part of my storehouse and sure enough, one day about a week after we came back from Chicago, I had a chance to depend on them. Liz, our last child, was about to leave home for college. Separation of any kind has always been difficult for me, no matter who leaves or for what reason. As I was beginning to catch signs of my separation anxieties I whispered aloud the words, "Surely I will be with you always." In my heart I put the emphasis on "I." And it helped. The words penetrated my fear and left me safe.

I was closing in on the difference between Manna Verses and Arsenal Verses.

- Manna Verses emphasize the oddly elusive nature of our relationship with God. We need to come to Him daily for a new supply of Himself. We can't capture Him, box Him. The poet Robert Frost once told Tib and me that he didn't like to try pinning down God with words. "It would be like pinning down a butterfly," he said. "If you do that you don't have a butterfly anymore."

- Arsenal Verses, paradoxically, emphasize the opposite. God's word is also imperishable, inexhaustible and eternal, and it can be stored up just as swords can be stored in an arsenal.

- Manna Verses are evidence of God's moment-by-moment closeness. He is up-to-date on what happens in our lives, and says so by highlighting His involvement verse for each day of our lives.

- Arsenal Verses are evidence of God's unchangeability, of the permanent quality of His truth.

- To depend on either Manna or Arsenal Verses alone is to leave out an important part of God's provision.

- Both Manna and Arsenal Verses are of God's choosing. He will highlight a Manna Verse on a page, or bring to mind an Arsenal Verse which He knows will best fit our grip.

· God supplies the spiritual energy in both experiences, too. The energy of a Manna Verse comes from the evidence of His caring, as when He tells us He is near, and loves us, or at times when He tells us that He disapproves of what we do. The energy of an Arsenal Verse comes from another kind of caring, as when we call on Him to do battle for us through the immense power of His word.

· Of course a Manna Verse can become an Arsenal Verse and vice versa. Any verse in the Bible can be either or both. When God gives a Manna Verse, if it has an unusual heft and balance and was given for a need that is likely to re-occur, why not memorize it and store it away?

6

Memorizing

*B*ut it was right here, at this point of memorization, that I ran into real trouble.

When I became convinced that Arsenal Verses were a necessary part of handling of problems, I made an inventory of the verses which I had at my disposal right then. Pitiful.

I've mentioned three. I could add another dozen, perhaps, but that exhausted my supply. I had not come from a tradition which emphasized learning the Bible. But that's not the real problem. The fact of the matter is that I have a very poor memory.

Scene: Tib and I are taking a course in French literature. Tib and I are to give a dialogue in class. I study my part diligently. Tib and I stand together in front of our fellow students. Tib delivers her opening line, then waits for me to pick up on her cue. She waits. And waits. She glances from me to the teacher in confusion. It is disaster for both of us, because I cannot remember a single word.

Scene: Greenwich Village, New York. It is many years later and I have been asked to take part in another play. Our then-teenaged son Scott has a friend, Chuck Nyren, who is a fledgling film producer. Chuck and Scott have written a screenplay. One part calls for a detective to enter a Greenwich Village apartment. He is wearing a raincoat. The detective—played by John Sherrill—is to shake water from his coat and speak the single line, "Well, I think we've got him."

This is such a simple scene, there is no need to rehearse. Chuck has turned his floodlights on. The camera is rolling. Perhaps it is all the wires, the confusion, the sudden expectant quiet. I step through the door all right. I shake imaginary rainwater from my collar. I try to remember my line. The camera rolls. And rolls. And rolls…

⸺ ⸺ ⸺ ⸺

How do you memorize if you have a leaky memory? Donn, when he was in high school, had brought home a book called, "How to Study." I got it out of the library, now, remembering that it had a chapter dealing with memorization.

There were, apparently, two keys. The first was repetition. The second was to spot whether you were a visual or oral learner. My basic orientation is visual. So I had the seemingly simple task of selecting Bible verses, writing them out and repeating them until they were mine.

Every day for several months I wrote out a new Bible verse on a 3 x 5 card and stuck it in my shirt pocket. Then, at random points through the day—while stopping at a traffic light, or sitting in a dentist's office, or waiting for the person I was calling to pick up the telephone—I would repeat the verse, then check my card to see how accurate I had been. Not very.

As the book suggested, I developed a follow-up system. Keying the cyclical repetition to my desk calendar, I reviewed the verse every third day, then every seventh day, then every month. And sure enough I was anchoring a few verses. But still, if I am to be honest, many more got away from me.

And then, at last, I discovered a secret.

One day I was having lunch with a man who held the key to a story I was interested in. "I think maybe I can help you," the man said. "Let me give you my home phone number."

With that he took out of his pocket a pencil and paper and handed them to me. I picked up the pencil absently, but when the man gave me his ten-digit number I did not write it down.

"Have you got that?" he asked.

"Oh yes."

"Without writing it down?"

"Don't worry, I won't forget it."

The man took back his pencil commenting that he wished he had a good memory like mine.

A good memory! I had been telling myself that I could not recall a thing. Yet here I was, confident that I could remember these ten numbers at will.

The key, I decided on reflection, was that my mind held on to things that were vital to me. I had very little trouble remembering the Manna Verses given to me most mornings, for I had learned from experience that these verses were going to be significant during the day. Since I knew they'd be important I could remember them without difficulty.

When it came to Arsenal Verses, however, I was in a different position. I had been trying to learn verses which only might *someday* turn out to be useful.

So I set about supplying myself with Arsenal Verses in a different way.

First, I limited my goal. I settled for a select store of weapons in battle-ready shape. Surely that was manageable, even for me.

Second, with a few exceptions, I learned short selections, not only because they were easier to memorize but also because they worked better. Even when I learned longer passages, it was short *portions* of the passage that did the fighting.

Third, and most important, I learned verses that met specific, current needs. A relationship was in trouble; I was struggling with a destructive emotion; work was not going right; one of the children was taking a long car trip; my priorities were out of line; a friend was facing an operation...I knew that the Bible would speak to each such need. So as I met the situations I stopped and looked until I found a Bible verse to fit. Then I memorized that verse. (If you are used to a particular edition of the Bible, it's probably better to memorize verses from that version. It makes memorization less difficult.)

At last I was under way. All these verses were not easy for me to learn, but learn them I did. They are mine forever now, and I use them all the time. I've made a list of my particular arsenal in the back of this book. Of course each person's battlegrounds, and therefore choice of weapons, will be different.

But there was one dynamic still to be explored, in the art of using these Manna and Arsenal Verses. And that was how best to release the power that lay coiled within them waiting to be used.

7

The Partnership of Power

*B*oth Manna and Arsenal Verses have the power to alter situations. But that power remains latent until it is released, as I discovered one evening.

There is a popular theory that a strange "pecking order" exists among people, similar to an order which can be found in a barnyard. A dominant rooster pecks another. He pecks a hen; she pecks on still another hen below her in the order. And so it goes right down to the bottom. I've observed this in myself. For reasons that resist understanding, I imagine myself below some people in the human pecking order, and above others.

I noticed it, for instance, one evening when Tib and I were visiting a writer who lives in nearby Connecticut. I admired Philip too much to be at ease with him. It was one of those excessive admirations that left me a little in awe. Philip was *too* talented, too surefooted, too witty. He chose other giants for his friends, which left me out.

Now we were moving into the dining room where Philip's housekeeper (naturally, I found this setup the height of glamour) had prepared a welcoming meal. As we were settling down I remembered something. Weeks ago in another context altogether I had stored away a short Arsenal Verse, from Acts 10:34 (KJV), "God is no respecter of persons"—God shows no partiality. He plays no favorites. There the Arsenal Verse lay, but that's as far as I got. Just then the housekeeper arrived with the soup; my attention was distracted.

Until, that is, just after supper when Philip took us for a stroll along his own private lakefront. I was in the process of feeling that this was surely the most favored of all writer's havens when *again* the verse from Acts 10:34 came to mind.

"Wait a minute," I said to myself while Tib carried the conversation. "Just *having* that verse isn't enough." It lay there, I went on thinking, filled with wonderful latent power, but just possessing it did not automatically release that power into my awkwardness. I had to go into partnership, *do* something, actively take a step, in order to release the dynamic potential within that verse. Otherwise, I suppose, if God did everything automatically, He would be violating my free will. My will had to be involved in order to complete the circuit.

"God is no respecter of persons," I said.

"What's that, John?" said Philip. "You'll do what?"

"…uh…excuse me…" But Philip was already off again following his own thoughts. *God is no respecter of persons,* I said again, pronouncing the words with my lips, as if saying them aloud. God does not see Philip as "higher" or "lower" than I am. God is not partial. Philip is just Philip, with his own talents and problems. Philip is Philip with weaknesses and strong points. He is Philip and I am John.

Well I can report that a change began that same night. I felt more at ease with the man. Tib did not have to do all the talking anymore. And ever since then it has been far easier to get along with myself when I'm around Philip. Later, the miracle occurred again in a relationship where I myself was "higher" on that strange and artificial pecking order. I found I could break the order down with the same Arsenal Verse no matter where I stood on the scale. I could be just plain John. But again I had to say the verse aloud or as close to aloud as the social situation permitted.

What exactly was happening here? I recalled how a Manna Verse came to my aid when I was tempted to cheat on a royalty report; I had repeated the protecting verse aloud on that occasion. I remembered when I sat down with Stan, my bachelor friend whose creativity was bottled up; there too I had spoken the Bible verse aloud. Was there something special in actually speaking a verse out? It was the American poetess Emily Dickinson who said,

> *A word is dead*
> *When it is said,*
> *Some say.*
> *I say it just*
> *Begins to live*
> *That day.*

Was speaking forth the creative principle that converted latent power into actual power? (Italics are added in the following verses.)

- "And God *said,* Let there be light: and there was light" (Genesis 1:3 KJV). The saying forth came before the manifestation.

- "If you confess *with your lips* that Jesus is Lord...you will be saved" (Romans 10:9 RSV). To "confess" in this sense means to "say with" God. When I confess God's word I am pronouncing His own word with Him.

- The spoken-out word had God's promise of effectiveness. "So shall my word be that *goes forth from my mouth*; it shall not return to me empty, but it shall accomplish that which I purpose..." (Isaiah 55:11 RSV).

- "The centurion replied, 'Lord, I do not deserve to have you come under my roof. But just say the word, and my servant will be healed'" (Matthew 8:8 NIV). The centurion knew that Jesus had the power, *provided* it was sent forth.

- "For he *spoke, and it came to be;* he commanded, and it stood firm" (Psalm 33:9 NIV).

All of these examples characterized Jesus' own experience in the wilderness.

My daily lectionary readings had brought Tib and me to Luke 4 where Jesus is tempted in the wilderness. Three times in a row He faced His trials by using Scripture in this same "Speaking-Forth Principle." He showed how to turn a "Latent Power" verse into "Actual Power." From His store of Scripture, He exploded Satan's luring suggestions by aiming one perfect word at the argument, then releasing its incredible power by speaking it forth.

Of all the principles I had encountered to date, this was perhaps the most important.

The Spirit took the first step in this cooperative effort by singling out verses to be used. He alone knew the complexities that surrounded a situation. He highlighted a passage or brought a memorized verse freshly to mind.

But then an act on my part was required.

I had to take this verse and apply it.

I had to speak it—preferably aloud—into the situation.

But when I did, as Jesus' temptations promised, miracles of power ensued.

8

Scripture Must Balance Scripture

I can well remember a traumatic little event that happened when our son Scott was fifteen.

On that morning, Scott was not in the house; he was on an overnight camping trip. Tib and I were having breakfast when we received a phone call from a neighbor with the news that he had seen Scott, a few days earlier, driving our family car down a nearby country lane. Was he sure it was *Scott?* Yes. When was this again? Two, three days ago. Well, thanks for letting us know.

Tib and I sat there letting our eggs grow cold as we tried to come to grips with our anger and puzzlement. What were we going to do? Scott had been so anxious to drive that I had occasionally talked him through the controls of a car, but always with the explicit instructions that he was never, never to touch those controls unless I was actually with him.

Now he had deliberately disobeyed. On one point Tib and I were united: we had to have a definite plan of action ready by the time Scott arrived home at five.

This whole misadventure took place in the early days of our experiments with the Bible, so I found myself wondering if we

could find a good Scriptural guideline. Sure enough, the shadow of
a verse came to mind.

Wasn't there an instruction that said you were not to get your
children angry? I got the concordance down from its shelf and
looked up the word *children*. Sure enough, there was my verse:

> *Fathers, do not exasperate your children; instead, bring them
> up in the training and instruction of the Lord.*
> *Ephesians 6:4* NIV

Well, that seemed clear enough. We should not provoke Scott to
wrath. That would mean going easy on him I supposed…good. I
was relieved. I never have been good at confrontations, because I am
afraid of my own anger. Perhaps I could just pray with the boy and
show him God's way.

Yet I was uncomfortable. Just the week before I'd heard a sermon on discipline. Hadn't the preacher quoted *another* Scripture
verse to the effect that although disciplining was never easy to go
through, it produced good results.

Uneasily—because I didn't really want to find it—I flipped
through the concordance again until I came to the word *discipline*,
and shortly I found this second reference too. I turned to the chapter in Hebrews and read this unwelcome passage:

> *No discipline seems pleasant at the time, but painful. Later
> on, however, it produces a harvest of righteousness and peace
> for those who have been trained by it.*
> *Hebrews 12:11* NIV

According to this verse I was to have no hesitation in disciplining Scott for this breach of rules. Hard as the correction was, it
would later produce "peaceful fruit."

My heart sank. If I followed this verse I couldn't avoid the
showdown.

So I was confused. The verses seemed to give opposite instructions. Throughout the day Tib and I talked over our dilemma, but

we couldn't come up with any good way to tell which verse we should follow. It wasn't that one was the word of God, while the other was secular wisdom; both were Scriptural. It wasn't even that one was from the New Testament and the other from the Old; both were from the Epistles.

In the end, we disciplined Scott. He was grounded and had to come home immediately after school for a month. But we announced the discipline without flying off the handle. Although it was hard on everyone during those weeks, we knew we had done the right thing.

There is a principle here taught by my friends Ross and Margaret Tooley of Youth With A Mission. *Scripture must balance Scripture.* "Just because the Bible says, in one passage, that we should take a certain action," they explain, "that does not free us from the obligation to seek guidance elsewhere in the Bible. Scripture must interpret Scripture. The Bible is not just 'Thus says the Lord,' but 'Thus *also* says the Lord.' To seek guidance without this balance is like trying to row a boat with one oar missing."

9

Getting Specific—
Even Though I'd Rather Not

Interlude

*B*y now I could see that it is possible to make friends with the Bible. I could bring myself to it and expect the Spirit to talk to me through its pages. It was an intimate communion where God would support, defend, and correct.

Of course, making friends with the Bible didn't happen in a vacuum. It took place in terms of a real life—in this case, my own. The life I've described so far has dealt with homey matters such as dogs and cars and real estate cheats.

But there were other areas that couldn't be handled in a day. Darker, more unyielding areas that I brought with me into my Christian life from before I saw Jesus in that hospital room. Jarring and jolting terrain that kept throwing me off balance. Ground which I was afraid to talk about, because I feared I would be scandalizing some people, or causing others to say, "What's he trying to do, be a little tin saint?"

The point is that, here too, the experiences I am going to describe were my own. My problems were in the areas of sex, competition, over-indulgence and fear. Someone else's will be different, but I suspect that we would share in common the fact that we have, in our make-up, stubborn fortresses whose lords don't give up easily.

The Bible had proven itself a friend in simpler, day-to-day problems. Would it also prove a companion-at-arms against these tougher enemies?

Problems Are Temptations

As I began to explore this question I found myself being drawn again and again to one portion of the Bible, the Temptation of Jesus. At first I thought this was just a personal preference. But then I began to suspect that the Temptation was not pulling me to itself just because I had testings of my own.

Perhaps the Temptation was God's Master Plan for handling problems?

If so, I was still missing something in that reading. So one bright morning with sunlight streaming through our living room window, I sat down again trying to come to grips with the elusive deeper meaning to the Temptation story. I read carefully:

> *And Jesus, full of the Holy Spirit, returned from the Jordan, and was led by the Spirit for forty days in the wilderness, tempted by the devil. And he ate nothing in those days; and when they were ended, he was hungry. The devil said to him, "If you are the Son of God, command this stone to become bread."*
> *And Jesus answered him, "It is written, 'Man shall not live by bread alone.' "*
> *And the devil took him up, and showed him all the kingdoms of the world in a moment of time, and said to him, "To you I will give all this authority and their glory; for it has been delivered to me, and I give it to whom I will. If you, then, will worship me, it shall all be yours."*
> *And Jesus answered him, "It is written,*
> *'You shall worship the Lord your God,*
> *and him only shall you serve.' "*

And he took him to Jerusalem, and set him on the pinnacle of the temple, and said to him, "If you are the Son of God, throw yourself down from here; for it is written,
  'He will give his angels charge of you, to guard you,'
  and
  'On their hands they will bear you up
  lest you strike your foot against a stone.'"
And Jesus answered him, "It is said, 'You shall not tempt the Lord your God.'" And when the devil had ended every temptation, he departed from him until an opportune time. And Jesus returned in the power of the Spirit into Galilee...
                                              Luke 4:1-14 RSV

A remarkable thing happened to me as I followed this account. *Two* different verses were highlighted.

The first was, "And Jesus, full of the Holy Spirit, returned from the Jordan, and was led by the Spirit for forty days in the wilderness, tempted by the devil" (verse 1).

The second came thirteen verses later. "And Jesus returned in the power of the Spirit into Galilee..." (verse 14).

I copied the two verses out in longhand, and it was in doing this that I noticed a striking similarity between them:

Jesus went into the wilderness full of the Spirit. He came out of the wilderness still in the Spirit.

Jesus remained in the Spirit, no matter what happened. This, I recalled, was the crucial signal by which John the Baptist could know that he had found Christ. John was to watch for one man on whom the Holy Spirit would descend and remain (John 1:33). Descend and *remain.* No other man in history had lived in such a way that the Spirit descended on him, and stayed with him always.

To stay in the Spirit—I was sure of it now—was the real problem Jesus faced in the wilderness.

The wilderness did not offer three different temptations as I'd always thought. It offered one. A single temptation; in the shape of different problems, to be sure, but a single testing just the same. The problems were in the area of His physical body (when He was hungry after a prolonged fast); in the area of His soul—His mind, emotions, affections (in questions involving His work); and in the area of His spirit (when He was offered a spiritual shortcut).

For Jesus, the problems were all temptations. Each had a common denominator. Each tried, with its particular pressures, to lure Him away from the Spirit.

What Does It Mean to Be "in the Spirit"?

When I tried to communicate this to Tib, though, I ran into a problem. "What do you mean by 'in the Spirit'?" she asked.

"Well...you know...in the *Spirit*."

"I couldn't tell you what the phrase means, though. Can you?"

"No."

So, before I could go any further, I had to come to grips more precisely with this term. Paul says we should "Walk in the Spirit..." (Galatians 5:16 KJV). John said that he was "...in the Spirit" on the Lord's day (Revelation 1:10 KJV). Jesus returned from the wilderness "in the power of the Spirit..." (Luke 4:14 KJV). What was the experience conveyed in this phrase?

I had a hint from my own life. After my conversion, and later after my Baptism in the Holy Spirit I was, for a few weeks or months, "in the Spirit." That is, I lived for a time in an exhilarating realm. Life was aglow. People were aglow. For a short while I was living so far above my problems that I couldn't see them.

But we don't live forever in such a state, not here on earth. I came down from my heaven and began to realize that problems were still here. That first-blush euphoria bore the same relationship to the *walk* in the Spirit that a honeymoon bears to *marriage*.

So I had to dig some more, and I did so by asking friends who might have hard experience behind their answers, what they included in the concept, "in the Spirit." Here is what I gleaned:

· To be in the Spirit is to become conscious, for a higher percentage of time, of God's continuing presence in our lives.

· To be in the Spirit is to be in the flow of His vital life and power.

· To be in the Spirit involves a quality of living, because the Fruit of the Spirit is growing:

> *The fruit of the Spirit is love, joy, peace, patience, kindness, goodness, faithfulness, gentleness, self control...*
> *Galatians 5:22,23* RSV

· To be in the Spirit is to exist in a different realm, where a miracle is not a surprise.

· There, in the realm of the Spirit, we have available the Gifts of the Spirit, ours to use as problems and opportunities present themselves.

> *To one there is given through the Spirit the message of wisdom, to another the message of knowledge by means of the same Spirit, to another faith by the same Spirit, to another gifts of healing by that one Spirit, to another miraculous powers, to another prophecy, to another distinguishing between spirits, to another speaking in different kinds of tongues, and to still another the interpretation of tongues.*
> *1 Corinthians 12:8-10* NIV

· To be in the Spirit is to be in the Kingdom of God for a given moment of time. Gordon Lyle, an investment counselor from Westport, Connecticut, sums it up this way. You are in the kingdom—in the Spirit—when you are:

—most fully yourself
—doing what the Father wants you to be doing
—using the tools He wants you to use
—when He wants you to use them
—where He wants you to be
—for His own purposes

All this was inherent in the expression "in the Spirit."

No wonder Satan wanted to seduce Jesus away from this position. All of the temptations he threw at Jesus were aimed at that same goal. Satan took problems and shaped them into temptations. Each problem became a red herring, trying to attract His attention. Satan forever tempted Him (as he tempts us all) to move out of the Spirit by turning toward the problem instead of toward the Father.

I wondered if I would ever be able to handle problems the way Jesus did. Could I learn to treat all problems as the single temptation to move out from the Spirit?

My problems themselves might, or might not, go away. That, apparently, was not Jesus' main concern. The issue was not to solve problems, or to avoid them, but to handle them in the Spirit.

And the way Jesus did this, without exception, was through Scripture.

10

Red Herring No. 1: Physical Problems

Jesus was hungry. Satan tempted Him to meet this physical problem by commanding the stones which lay around Him so abundantly to be turned into bread.

Real as it was, the problem with hunger was an issue which was meant to distract. Satan tried to get Jesus to focus on His physical needs, but Jesus saw the ruse as a temptation to shift His gaze away from the face of the Father. That was the real problem: staying in constant touch with the Father.

Jesus handled this temptation by depending on Scripture. Against the suggestion of Satan, He immediately used the word of God. It was the only weapon He used even though He could have turned to other powers available to Him—miracles, angels, prayer. Of all His resources, He chose to lean only on the Scripture given to Him specifically for this occasion.

I came down the stairs in our little, somewhat-Tudor house in Oxford, England, determined not to let my anxiety show. Tib had set breakfast in our "sunny" living room. Actually, the sun was only wishfulness, for the July skies were colored orange-gray again by smog from the industrial belt that surrounded Oxford. But I wasn't going to let that get at me today.

Tib and I were living in England on a year-long writing assignment. Only our youngest, Liz, was with us. Scott was out of college, married now, and living with his wife Meg in New Hampshire; Donn was at the University of Madrid in Spain; he would be joining us here next month.

We certainly had every reason to believe that we were where the Lord wanted us. He had provided this house, for example, when real estate agents said none were available.

Yet as I came down the last stair that morning and headed into the living room for my favorite breakfast of kippers-and-poached, Tib took one look at me and asked what was wrong. Nothing. Was I sure? Certainly.

With an excellent show of cheerfulness, it seemed to me, I left our house and started my morning walk down to the office. Our house did not have enough room for Tib and me both to have work space there, so I had rented a room in a private home in central Oxford. The idea of walking the mile and a half each way each day seemed a good one at first. But I soon discovered why Oxford has a reputation for bad air. Although the city is best known for its university, Oxford is also a major automobile manufacturing center. Convoys of transport trucks move in and out, spitting their choking diesel foulness into the air. Because Oxford sits in a shallow valley, the septic air cannot escape. I quickly discovered that trying to get to my office by the main road meant fighting diesels all the way. I would have abandoned walking altogether if I had not discovered the canal.

Hidden behind a row of houses in Oxford is a stretch of old barge canal, dating back to the days before the railroad. The canal, used now mostly for holiday barges, flowed right past the backyard of my office. So each morning I walked the towpath, past old boatyards and lush playing fields where schoolboys were intent on their soccer games.

Now, on this morning when I had told Tib nothing was wrong, I walked along my towpath trying to keep as calm as the swans that slid along the water beside me. But I wasn't calm. I tried humming. That was a mistake. Three bars into the melody and I had to stop, clear my throat, try again, stop again. The panic that rode my spine and exploded in my brain was not to be stilled by a song.

For persistent hoarseness is one of the classic danger signs of cancer.

I had been trying for two months to ignore the signals. If you paid attention to every little cough… But programming my thoughts didn't work. My mind insisted on snapping back to my two previous cancer battles, and that morning as I passed a humpbacked bridge on the canal I admitted at last that I was afraid.

And I knew the name of the fear, too. Pain. Not death, but pain. Ironically, although after Marc Hall's prayers at our church my surgeon had found only dried up nodules on my neck, although the cancer had been healed by the Lord, still I had very nearly died on the operating table when my lungs collapsed under anesthesia. Now, I relived the memory of waking up in the recovery room so pierced by pain that I clawed my way out of bed, pulling at all the doctors' wires and tubes. Nurses dashed up, pushed me down, inserted hypodermics. As I went out, I was saying to myself, "Never. I won't go through this again."

So that July morning I went to my office in Oxford, all right, but I didn't get much done. Instead of working I stared out the window. Eleven thirty came. Good, it was time for lunch. I walked down to the corner and ordered a leisurely Pakistani meal. No reason to hurry. When I returned I was drowsy and decided on a short snooze. I put my head down on the table then awoke to doodle for a while. Then it was time to go home.

This became my pattern. Although I had put a name to my fears, I still did not worry aloud. I did not tell Tib. I did not go to the doctor, who might confirm what I suspected. I did drop into church on my way home from work one day, but the empty and cold sanctuary seemed to capture the sound of my cough and throw it back at me.

I shunned Scripture as effectively as I avoided Tib. I hid from both with the only successful play-acting I had ever achieved. Or at least I thought it was successful, because both Tib and God let me go my lonesome way for a while. I continued to talk to Tib about the weather and what I had for lunch, and plans for meeting Donn's plane when he came in from Spain in a few days. It was talk without communication.

It was the same with the Bible. Tib and I did continue to read selections from the morning lectionary, but I discovered, those days, how easy it is to read the Bible and not hear it at all.

What I did do, in contrast, was to step out of the Spirit altogether. I disappeared into excellent British television, and into wine. A sallow-faced man kept a Wine and Spirits Shoppe a few blocks from our home, and it was a rare evening that did not see me stopping for a bottle, or so, of claret.

Then one night Tib and I went to the Bear Hotel in Woodstock, just outside of Oxford. The Bear is our favorite hotel in the world, and that night we splurged by ordering the house specialty, Blenheim partridge.

Toward the middle of the meal, Tib leaned forward.

"I don't think you're playing fair with me."

I took a bite of the partridge and ate in silence. Tib wouldn't help me out. She said nothing more. Finally, I spoke the words I should have said months ago.

"You're right. I'm scared."

"What is it John?"

"Well," I cleared my throat once again and took another large swallow of claret. "Well, for a couple of months I've had this hoarseness in my throat and trouble swallowing and it's getting worse."

It all came out in a rush. Once I had started, I found myself telling Tib about the first day I'd noticed it, walking beside my canal. I told her about the empty, workless days, about my determination to carry the fear by myself. Tib's dinner sat on her plate, untouched from the moment I started my confession.

"...no, it's excellent...it's just that I'm not hungry," Tib was explaining to the head waiter.

"You see I was right," I said as the waiter left us, "I shouldn't have dumped this on your shoulders. I want you to *promise* you won't tell anyone else. Not the kids. Or our mothers. Not even the prayer group."

As far as I can recall, only once in our lives has Tib simply ignored my wishes. That same evening, without telling me of course, she wrote to our prayer group back in New York, telling them exactly what was happening.

At Tib's insistence I began making inquiries, trying to find the best head-and-neck specialist in the United Kingdom. The result was an appointment with a top specialist. The hour was fixed for eleven o'clock Wednesday morning a week away.

Suddenly we had seven days of hard waiting on our hands. We'd originally planned a vacation during this time. Donn and I have birthdays on August 1 and August 2. Donn was flying in tomorrow from Spain. Liz's school year was over. We had planned to celebrate all these occasions at once by taking a week-long do-it-yourself trip on the Thames in a small river launch.

"Do you think we should just go ahead?" Tib asked as we drove to the airport to pick up Donn.

I shrugged. Why not? I didn't think I could take a week of just waiting around. We also discussed whether or not to bring Donn and Liz in on our problem. After all, we didn't know yet that the fear was based on reality. But was reality the criterion? Or was the fact that I was afraid, by itself, enough?

Next morning our gear was stowed aboard *Wingo*, with its tiny galley, four narrow bunks and mini-deck aft. The launch was snugly moored to a tree at the boatyard on the River Thames at Oxford. I'd had very little experience with boats, but nonetheless Donn and Liz and Tib and I climbed aboard with great confidence. After all, the owner himself had seemed satisfied a little while ago when he had taken us out to show me the controls.

I eased the throttle forward, nosed the boat out into that current, and promptly found myself swinging in circles.

All that afternoon the rigors of learning how to handle *Wingo* were so time-consuming that we had no opportunity to bring up the subject of cancer.

But at last it was evening. We moored against a steep, chiseled bank along the Thames. Supper was over. A rare, warm evening let us linger outdoors on the rear deck. A swan family sailed by, not even acknowledging us with a turn of the head. In the distance across the tableland farms of Oxfordshire, a country churchbell sounded. It was the right time.

I told the kids. I told them about the hoarseness, the fears, the loneliness. I told them of the upcoming visit to the specialist and of our hopes that it would be a good report. Tib confessed she had written the prayer group, and I found I was glad. Tib even had a reply from our friend Jean Nardozzi which she now read. Jean said a lot of people were praying for us; she chided me for keeping my fear secret and urged us to stay close to the Bible.

"Then let's do it," said Donn.

Tib got out the lectionary. I explained to the kids where I was now in this adventure with the Bible; how before I started running scared I had been learning to let the Bible speak to me.

"Maybe that could happen now," Liz suggested. I hoped so. Tib and Donn and Liz read while I listened. Tib started with a Psalm. Nothing. Then Donn read a passage from Jeremiah. Nothing. Then Liz began the eighth chapter of Romans. Still nothing was happening. I wondered if I was in for another of those times when the Bible would not speak, when suddenly there it was. How well I remember Liz's clear, soft, still slightly tearful voice. She read, "For you did not receive the spirit of slavery to fall back into fear..." (Romans 8:15 RSV).

I sat up straighter. That was my verse! I asked Liz to read it again. As she spoke I realized that this was *exactly* what a consuming fear produced; a spirit of slavery. I was bound by it, and wanted release. I told the kids what I was finding out about converting Latent Power into Actual Power by speaking forth a verse. Then, there on our boat I put into practice the principle Jesus taught in the wilderness.

"All right, Lord," I said. "I'm going to move to the attack. I know this verse is mine, and I take it up as the only weapon I need. I claim this as Your own voice speaking a fact. 'I did not receive the spirit of slavery to fall back into fear, but I have received the spirit of sonship.' Lord, I speak that fact forth."

To say that I had no problem staying in God's presence after that would, of course, be simplistic. I did have bolts of fear thrown at me, and the fear did grab my attention, diverting it from God. The difference was that now I also had a weapon to throw against the fear, allowing me to move back quickly into the Spirit. Every time I was attacked, I did one thing only, and I did it instantly. I stated my fact. *For you did not receive the spirit of slavery to fall back into fear, but you received the spirit of sonship.* I thanked the Lord for that fact. That's all I did. Nothing more. No arguing, no analyzing. I just said that Power Verse into the fear, and it went away. Temporarily, but it did go away. When it returned, I repeated my defense in childlike simplicity.

All I can say is that the rest of our week on the Thames was almost one hundred percent sheer, abandoned joy. We laughed. We ate well and often. We moored the boat and went on long walks. At the last possible minute we headed back.

Yes, we all agreed, it had been a marvelous trip. I did not know what the result of the doctor's examination was going to be next day, but I'd reached that wonderful place where—at least as far as this situation was concerned—staying in the Spirit did not depend on my problem's being solved.

⟣ ⟣ ⟣ ⟣

It was Wednesday. Eleven in the morning. All of us—Tib and Donn and Liz and I—were sitting in the uncomfortable waiting room of London's ancient, red brick hospital which specializes in cancer and related conditions.

My name was called.

Two hours followed of swallowing strange material, being strapped on a machine and turned upside down, submitting to thumps and whacks and tongue depressors and blood specimens and X-rays and tests I couldn't fathom at all.

"Would you all like to be together when I give you the report?" the doctor asked at the end of all of this.

"Yes." The doctor took us into his office, set us down in a circle... and then smiled.

"I know how worried you must be. But I have the best of reports for you. I can find absolutely nothing wrong."

A too-good-to-be-true silence.

"You live in Oxford don't you?" the doctor asked.

"That's right."

"And for how long?"

I counted back. "Eight months."

"It generally takes four for throat symptoms to appear." The doctor shook his head. "It's the Oxford air. I shouldn't be surprised if that city's air is the worst in the world. Oxford will make the healthiest of us cough, and you seem to be unusually susceptible. You're suffering from simple twentieth-century pollution."

～～ ～～

We stopped at the first restaurant we came to. It had sidewalk tables. There we celebrated with a victory dinner, but even as we ate I knew we had already celebrated the real victory, aboard *Wingo*. As I was enjoying myself I got to thinking. My physical problem had been in the area of health. But it could have been in any area that touches our physical lives: overweight, trying to get along on too little money, or even just some feature of our appearance we don't like. All are red herring problems in that they demand so much attention they can take us away from what should be the focus of our lives. The problems are real, but they mask a greater problem; in Satan's hands they become temptations to take our eyes off God.

I wish I could say that the principles I had been learning so painfully, now carried over automatically to the next problem-temptation I faced.

Unfortunately that is not the case.

11

Red Herring No. 2: Problems in Our Work

Jesus had work to do. Important work which had been given Him by the Father.

But this very fact gave the devil an opportunity to attack. Satan knew that he could make this work go faster and—to all appearances—better. He could effectively and efficiently deliver to Jesus all the kingdoms of the earth. Satan also knew that unless Jesus used his (Satan's) methods He would reach only a few people during His lifetime. That achievement would certainly not appear to be very spectacular.

"The way your work is done," Satan whispers, "is not so important as results. Let me help you and you'll get more done. Keep your eye on the outcome. That's all that really matters."

We all face this red herring of achievement. And it is especially subtle when our work is good, valuable and helpful to others. A woman is raising children; what could be more important? A man's company hires hundreds of people, scores of families depend for their livelihood on landing a certain contract. Still another has a "ministry" given him by God Himself. We often can honestly persuade ourselves that the success of our work is more important than how we achieve it.

In my own case, Tib and I were writing books which we hoped were important. The methods we used? Well, it's true that the methods were hurting us. But then…

We have good friends, Frank and Claire Coffin, who own a home on Nantucket Island. Every now and then Tib and I will go there off season for a few days of work away from the telephone. In the very early spring when it is still cold, before the summer residents come, Frank and Claire's house is so isolated that we can go for days with the low-hovering harriers as our only companions.

I was at the Coffins' place now. I had come alone this time because, in addition to a project for *Guideposts,* I had another kind of work to do. I'd come armed with a Power Verse, determined not to leave Nantucket until I had taken a step toward solving a serious problem which had been emerging slowly over the years in my working relationship with Tib.

"I want to apply Matthew 10:26 to my problem, Lord," I said; "'There is nothing concealed that will not be disclosed, or hidden that will not be made known.' Will You help me make manifest the things which are hurting us?"

⁂

The problem had come into focus one day months earlier when I went into Tib's office to sharpen a pencil. It should have been a moment for a pleasant visit. Sun poured onto her desk, leaving a pattern of colored light from the stained glass design she had hung in her window. The cat was curled up next to her. Papers were strewn about—always a good sign with Tib; the messier her desk, the better she is working.

The manuscript under her pen was the last draft I had done on *The Hiding Place.* Tib was concentrating and paid no attention as I stuck my pencil into the sharpener and began to grind away. She was so intent that she never looked up while I ground that poor pencil to a stub. My eyes followed the intricate, crossed out lines and rewritten portions of my draft. She was changing everything!

I said not a word, but as I left the room I knew that we were headed for trouble.

Later, while Tib, binoculars in hand, was off on her daily bird-walk, I went back to her office and looked at the manuscript more closely. She had rewritten heavily, not only on that page but on previous pages too. Of course she was supposed to be rewriting. My job on this manuscript was to tell the story; give the narrative a forward thrust. Tib was to take this draft of mine and work on characterization, emotional development and immediacy. My work usually came first in time sequence. Although it was a draft, it wasn't a rough draft. Long ago I discovered that it was important for me to turn over to Tib the very best work I was capable of. This meant doing two to four rewrites, however many it took before I began to spin wheels.

It had been a successful partnership in many ways. But over the past few years some of the flaws in this plan began to show up.

Our problem began in this way: For years book and magazine articles we worked on were edited without our names appearing on them, so the problem of identity never came up. The first book on which our names appeared was *The Cross and The Switchblade,* with David Wilkerson, which Tib and I wrote and signed together. Our second signed book was *They Speak With Other Tongues.* That project too started off as a joint by-line effort; both our names would be on it. It was to be an objective, somewhat distant, reporters' view of the pentecostal movement.

When the manuscript was just about finished, the unthinkable happened. I received the Baptism in the Holy Spirit myself. Our judicious, objective viewpoint was gone! We both felt there was nothing to do but toss away the first version and start again. Now, instead of a report we had a personal narrative. We tried to tell the story in the first person plural, but it didn't work, the search and the experience had to be told from the viewpoint of one person.

"And that person is you, John," Tib said. "I haven't had this experience yet, you have. You should tell the story." I agreed, too readily, as it turned out, and we wrote the story that way. In our own home we thought of the book as "ours," but that's not what people reading the story thought. The book had my name on it, so naturally it was John's. Tib assured me she had no problem with that.

The real problem followed when our other books also became "John's."

Once, I actually witnessed for myself the phenomenon Tib had to live with. We were at a conference together. I watched an intelligent-looking, well-groomed lady come up, carrying in her hand a copy of one of our books with "John and Elizabeth Sherrill" plainly printed on the jacket. The woman wrung Tib's hand. "This book of your husband's has meant so much to me!" she said. Tib, better at acting than I, exchanged a look with me then flashed a convincing smile of appreciation at the woman.

For years we knew that there was a terrible tension here. An unhappiness was building. In moments of high communication Tib would tell me what it was like to feel like a pane of window glass. "A smudged one, too, because I feel so guilty about reacting this way."

"I don't know why it should be starting to bother me now," she said to me one day as we drove in to a *Guideposts* meeting, "when I've worked anonymously for so many years. I've loved the privacy of not having my name on things. I think it's having become the-wife-of so much of the time that's getting to me. People need to be valued as *themselves*."

In the meanwhile, poison was setting in for me too. Long ago, in our own circle of writing friends, Tib's unique ability had become apparent. At the magazine we always turned to her when there was need for an especially sensitive story. Each month *Guideposts* surveyed a sampling of readers for reactions to stories: the most popular articles were those Tib had written or edited. Rising slowly to the threshold of consciousness was the fear that Tib was a better writer than I was. Like her, I knew that I *shouldn't* react this way. But in fact I am a very, very competitive person, and my own wife was emerging as a threat.

Even the way *The Hiding Place* came into our lives helped reveal some of my competitiveness. Tib met Corrie ten Boom while on a trip to Germany. It was love from the start. Tib came back flushed with excitement.

"I don't know whether I've done something wonderful or awful," she said as I drove her back from Kennedy Airport. "I've signed us up for a book."

I guess my face did show a certain blanched quality. So far, in the division of labor in our partnership, I had been the one to sign up the books. When Tib went on to outline the plot of Corrie's story to me, I was appalled. A middle-aged Dutch shopkeeper who was involved with the resistance movement in World War II? The story happened so long ago and so far away! Who would be interested in such a thing?

We should have decided then and there to let this be the first book Tib signed by herself. She suggested that, she says, although to this day I don't remember it. Was I, deep in my unconscious, telling her to get down and stay down?

In any event, I plunged ahead, blocked out the story, wrote scenes, developed the narrative thrust. For some reason though, I was reluctant to turn the story over to Tib. Instead of doing two or three drafts I did five. Over and over the story I went, determined, I suppose, to have it so good that Tib would say, "Well, there's really nothing for me to do."

Then came the day when the last page of my work came back from the typist. In a little ceremony I handed it over to Tib.

"Please be with Tib now, Lord, as she takes this manuscript and adds, subtracts, highlights, brings to it her special genius."

What a hypocritical prayer that was!

As the weeks passed and Tib did add her special genius, I began to make more and more frequent trips into her office to sharpen pencils.

Finally my anger came out all at once. Very often we get our best talking done in the car, and so it was this time. We were driving to Washington. We got no further than the oil refineries of New Jersey before I brought up with Tib how I really felt about the way the manuscript was being changed.

It wasn't a polite exposition. My feelings spewed out of me. Tib listened in silence as I accused her of destroying not only my work but me.

What were we going to do? We both realized that we had hit a deep-rooted personal issue. But in the meanwhile there was a book at stake. Corrie, then in her seventies, was eager for her book to come out as fast as possible. We had a realistic time factor to consider. We couldn't just shelve the project. So by the time we reached the Delaware Memorial Bridge, we had decided on a practical strategy. We would ask our long-time friend, Arthur Gordon, then a Roving Editor for the *Reader's Digest*, to look at our two versions, side by side.

It was an awkward position to ask any friend to step into. Anyone with less empathy for the plight of writers would simply have refused. But Arthur heard our hurt and opened himself up to a lot of work and possible misunderstanding. I will never forget the day we met, two weeks later, in the penthouse of the Yale Club in New York, to which Arthur belongs. Finally Arthur put our two manuscripts on the coffee table in front of him.

"There's no doubt that this is publishable," Arthur said, patting the version I had written. "It probably would do all right, too."

Then he put his hand on Tib's version. "But *this* now…" his eyes brightened, "…this work sings."

So, sitting now in the living room of Frank and Claire's house on Nantucket, I remembered how I had struggled out of my too-low chair at the Yale Club and walked around the room trying to handle my feelings. I put on my best good-sport manner. I told Tib she should feel free to do a complete rewrite on the manuscript without worrying about my feelings.

With my will I meant that. But as the weeks passed I began to realize that my emotions and my will were unrelated creatures. I couldn't fool Tib. Soon tension was building again. Our physical life together suffered. My work came to a stop. Even magazine articles, which I usually handled without trouble, became torture.

All right, I said to myself there in the Coffins' living room, where does this leave me? How should I face this problem? For one thing, it was clearly in the realm of work. We had "important" work to do, and for years we had let ourselves be persuaded that results came first. No matter what the cost in personal growth, no matter how snarled up our feelings were getting, results were what mattered.

"All right, Lord," I said. "Every problem offers a choice. I can move one step closer to You, or I can move one step away from You. I choose to move toward You. Please, before I leave this island, show me Yourself in this problem."

I asked God to show me Himself. He did, but not before He showed me myself, and He did it through a commonplace kitchen appliance.

To this day I marvel at what happened there in the Coffins' kitchen. Claire had a new appliance, a compactor, which compresses table scraps, wastepaper, even glass and tin cans into a small package which can then be disposed of. It is a useful device, especially out in the country where trash pickup is infrequent. Since the first hours of my visit here, six days ago, the machine had slowly been filling up.

Then one morning I looked into the can of coffee and realized that I was almost out. Now, the one thing which can stop me at my work is to run out of coffee. So I decided to drive into Nantucket Center to do some shopping.

But the car key wasn't on the marble front hall table where I was sure I had left it.

I looked in the bedroom, checked every jacket, emptied my pants pockets. Nothing. Had I left it in the car? No. Had I remembered to bring a spare key? Or was our extra key in the glove compartment? No.

By now I was worried. It would take days for Tib to mail a duplicate. I looked for another half hour then got around, at last, to asking for help. "Lord," I said, "would You please tell me where that key is?" It was a simple prayer and I had hardly finished it before my eyes fell on the compactor.

I opened the machine, bent over and looked inside. No key, of course. What a ridiculous idea! How could a car key fall into a trash compactor? How in fact could the key be in the kitchen at all since there was never any reason to bring it here. I lifted a lettuce leaf, laughing at myself. It was not exactly a pleasant task to go squishing around in crushed kitchen goo, but I picked up that lettuce leaf and looked. No key.

Of course, there wasn't! I turned away, intending to stop this search right there. But just then an incredible idea sprung to mind.

"Keep searching and you will find the key to your car and also the key to your problem."

I shook my head! What an odd thought. Yet I couldn't lose the feeling that the idea had come to me from God. So, despite all logic, I spread newspaper on the floor, rolled my sleeves up to the elbows, and with a sigh reached into that compactor.

Soon I had to start digging. What a mess. The deeper I got the more distasteful the waste became. Trash compacted on top of trash. Just like my problem with work, Lord?

Surely I wasn't supposed to take the parallel literally. Or was I?

I lifted out a smashed plastic tray from a carton of tomatoes. There goes the argument I had with Tib last week over final changes she was making in *The Hiding Place*. I removed a flattened wad of paper toweling. There goes the moment I had appropriated some of the applause that belonged to Tib.

Still I dug. There, as a crumpled aluminum tray from a TV dinner, go my anxieties about failure. Why did failure make me so uneasy? "You had to achieve in order to win love!" the Spirit whispered to me. "That is a lie you are uncovering. Keep digging. You are almost there."

One more layer of guck. I recognized the chicken dinner I had on my first night on the island six days ago. Now I was at the very bottom. It was runny, smelly, unpleasant work. I had long ago given up on the key. There was no way it could be under six days worth of refuse because I had used the car often since arriving, so even if by some freak chance the key *had* fallen into the compactor it couldn't be way down here. Why, then, was I continuing to dig? And why dig into the muck of my own past? Was it because, by the very process of bringing things to light, I was taking away their ability to damage?

⟞ ⟞ ⟞ ⟞

I leaned back, wiped my hands dry and remembered our most recent visit with Jamie Buckingham, who had come to New York to attend an editorial meeting at *Guideposts*. The visit came shortly after I began to have trouble with work. Each morning I'd sit down to those menacing rows of keys, each evening I'd get up with those keys largely unused.

That night after the meeting Tib and I drove Jamie to his hotel. In the car we told him about our battle over *The Hiding Place*, and about how I hadn't been able to work since Arthur's verdict on the two manuscripts. As we drew up in front of Jamie's hotel and parked, Jamie asked me, "What would happen if Tib wrote a book and signed it and you wrote a book and signed it and Tib's sold better?"

The answer I gave was intended to be flippant. "It would kill me," I said.

Silence from Jamie and Tib.

"And that," said Jamie at last, "is what Tib knows. For years she's known."

"Oh come on now, you guys. I'm joking."

"What you really want," said Jamie, ignoring my protest, "is to be *better* than Tib. Not equal to, but better."

Again there was silence. Truth had been spoken and there wasn't much else to say.

⟞ ⟞ ⟞ ⟞

"Why are you reminding me of that, Lord?" I asked. Apparently, in order to feel worthwhile I had to earn love by feeling *better* than other people? What a devastating insight. The drive to excel, a counselor had once suspected, dated back to childhood when I felt that to survive I had to be better than my sister. Taller, wiser, smarter, older. I still had the compulsion. I had to be bett*er* than Tib at writing. High*er* than someone else. I had to work hard*er* than other people. Was there no end to the "Er-thans"? "The Er-thans,

Lord, are my undoing. They are the bottom of the soggy mass of emotions and just about as unappealing as this soup in the bottom of the compactor."

Fascinated by the analogy, I stirred the muck now with a knife. And while I was stirring in the last of the unpleasant sludge, there at the ultimate bottom of the compactor, all alone except for the top of one tin can, shone the bright, beautiful car key.

I reached in and took it out and put it respectfully onto a paper towel. Unbelieving, I sat down.

It was an utterly silent moment there in that isolated hilltop in the Nantucket springtime.

I just sat there in the kitchen, holding the key in the palm of my hand, realizing that I was taking part in an unusual, acted-out conversation with God. It was a living parable. The automobile key had been in the garbage all along, and in some mysterious way I knew it. The key to my problems with Tib—the Er-than Syndrome—had been in the garbage of my mind all along, and in some mysterious way I knew that too.

I had come to the island with Matthew 10:26 (NIV) to speak into the work problem I was facing. "There is nothing concealed that will not be disclosed, or hidden that will not be made known." That word had been used to bring secrets to light, but now I needed another Power Verse which would help me drive away the "Er-thans" whenever they appeared.

I got out my Bible and opened it on the kitchen table. I turned to Luke 4 and re-read the account of Jesus' second problem-temptation.

> *And the devil, taking him up into an high mountain, showed unto him all the kingdoms of the world in a moment of time. And the devil said unto him, All this power will I give thee, and the glory of them: for that is delivered unto me; and to whomsoever I will I give it.*
> *If thou therefore wilt worship me, all shall be thine.*
> *Luke 4:5-7 KJV*

As I read, the three words *kingdom* and *power* and *glory* seemed to take on special importance. All three were claimed by Satan as his domain. Yet even that could be Satan's lie. Because there was another verse, the doxology at the end of the Lord's own prayer, that claimed all three for God: "For thine is the kingdom, and the power, and the glory" (Matthew 6:13 KJV).

That then would be my Arsenal Verse. The glory and the power of achieving did not belong to me. Any time I claimed them, I would be stepping out of the Kingdom, and into Satan's realm of lies.

Three years have passed since that experience with the compactor in Nantucket. The living parable remains as vivid in my memory as if it had happened yesterday.

How much has changed? The most important shift has come in my relationship with Tib. It is better across the board. We still have our lively disagreements—I'd worry if we didn't—but they are on specific issues and once finished they are out of the way. Our family life has never been so good. Our physical life has never been better.

And our work?

We may one day start writing together again, using different ground rules. But meanwhile, we decided that we ought to work independently. *The Hiding Place* was finished. Tib began thinking about a book she'd like to write alone. I reminded myself of the "thanksgiving" book I had determined to do after my cancer scare in England, where all royalties would belong to God.

What better subject for my first solo effort than these very discoveries I was making with the Bible?

And what better way to act on my new Arsenal Verse than to turn any profits over to Him? *"Thine* is the kingdom and the power and the glory!" So often the little kingdoms we carve out for ourselves are based, simply and bluntly, on money. "Money is power." "Money is safety." To one afflicted with the Er-than Syndrome, such slogans seemed all too believable.

By writing about the release I was finding in the Bible—and by accepting no money from the project—I could fling one of Satan's lies back in his face.

That same week, even before I left Nantucket, I began making notes for this book.

12

Red Herring No. 3: The Spiritual Attack

The most subtle of Satan's onslaughts in the Judean wilderness, he saved for last: the attack through the Word of God itself.

And he took him to Jerusalem, and set him on the pinnacle of the temple, and said to him, "If you are the Son of God, throw yourself down from here; for it is written,
*   'He will give his angels charge of you, to guard you,'*
*   and*
*   'On their hands they will bear you up*
*   lest you strike your foot against a stone.'"*
And Jesus answered him, "It is said, 'You shall not tempt the Lord your God.'"

Luke 4:1-14 RSV

I stood looking at myself in the bathroom mirror. Red lines wandered through my eyes. I had a heavy, bogged down feeling that I knew would interfere with the rest of my day.

It was no mystery what the trouble was. Simple overindulgence. Years ago we started a system in our family whereby first one, then the other of us would fix supper. When the boys were younger, their contribution was usually hamburgers or hotdogs. With Liz it might be hamburgers too, but the table would be set with her great-grandmother's china, candles, and from only-Liz-knew-where, a centerpiece.

Last night had been my turn. I started drinking early, while making the fish soup. By the time dinner was ready I had made a major assault on the bottle of Bernkastler.

Then there was wine with the meal too. Then wine with an hour in front of television. I chose Kojak rather than public television because there would be plenty of ad breaks, opportunities to slip out to the kitchen where I kept my supply of jug wine.

So that's why I stood in front of the mirror now, staring at my puffy eyes. And this wasn't before my conversion, it was fifteen years afterwards. Something was happening that I did not like at all.

Yet the use of wine, I reminded myself often, was Scriptural. The psalmist spoke of God's giving us "wine that maketh glad the heart of man…" (Psalm 104:15 KJV). Paul told Timothy to "use a little wine for thy stomach's sake…" (1 Timothy 5:23 KJV). Wine was the common table drink of Palestine. Jesus drank wine and He created it at the first miracle He ever performed.

Oh, I'd often heard the argument—both in Kentucky where I grew up and later in other parts of the country—that the wine of the Bible was unfermented. But this seemed out of kilter with life in the Near East. It was certainly out of keeping with the accepted ways of many twentieth-century European Christians.

Years before, Tib and I were visiting a friend in her seaside home in Georgia. Betty came from a missionary family where she had been exposed to the tradition that wine in the Bible was grape juice. But just before our visit Betty had had to take a second look at that understanding after returning from a trip to Europe. One night she had been invited to dine with a dedicated Swiss Christian family. At the table was a devout, grandmotherly lady. When Betty asked for water with her meal, this dear lady was *shocked*. Water!? And she expressed her shock with many of the same phrases Betty had heard applied to wine. A Christian drank *water* instead of wine?! Water wasn't good for the system. Wine was healthier, and more Scriptural too!

Here, for the first time in Betty's experience, in a familiar Bible-centered setting, wine was accepted as a sanctified part of normal living. Real wine, not an unfermented beverage.

And what about the Bible? When Betty returned to Georgia she took time to go through the Bible, looking up every reference to wine. "When I was finished," Betty told us, "it was clear to me that whatever else you can say about Bible wine, it isn't grape juice."

I was certain of this too. Still, something was nagging at me, saying that in my case it was not all right to drink wine. Efforts at moderation failed. One drink with meals? Not for me: once I started, I always ended up having more, often secretly, out in the kitchen. Occasionally I would take a bootstrap stand, throw away all our wine and stop drinking altogether. Our friends were confused. Whenever we were invited for dinner the first question was, "John, are you on or off?"

Tib was thoroughly aware of my struggle, so although she enjoyed wine greatly, whenever I stopped she would stop too. I remember once when she agreed to the brave stand of giving away our stemware. We made this gesture just before taking a sea-trip to Europe. Friends brought champagne to the sailing party on the QE2. With self-conscious willpower, I poured glasses of bubbly for others, while I drank ginger ale and Tib drank Perrier water.

That effort lasted exactly two hours longer. We had just settled down in the dining room when the wine steward came by. We knew MacNeil from previous trips. His face lit up at the sight of such good customers. Fingering the great brass key which hung around his neck, MacNeil leaned over our table and placed the plush carte in front of me. "What will you be eating tonight?"

It was his way of asking what wine we wanted. For a brief moment I battled. What about our forever decision? What about the sacrifice of Tib's stemware? And all that ginger ale still cloying in my mouth!

But then, this did seem like a more than special occasion. I leaned toward Tib. "Maybe just for the trip?"

"You'll have to decide, honey."

And it was all over. I looked up at MacNeil and told him we'd start with a little light Mosel. Within one day, my drinking pattern was back to its full-fledged overindulgence.

The change began on a trip to California. Air travel has always been my nemesis. Those long hours in the airport! The chrome chairs, the endless, clattering corridors, the airline meals which our daughter in-law Meg calls "plastic food units." It made time go faster to get aboard in a wine-glow, rather than to suffer the various indignities with my faculties in merciless focus. As usual, I arrived at the airport with enough time to assure a meal at the Skyview Restaurant, where I ordered lightly from the menu and heavily from the wine list.

When I got to the coast that evening I checked in at our favorite motel in the area, the Casa Malibu, an old fashioned bougainvillea-draped place right on the Pacific. I unpacked, prepared to follow my usual pattern of taking a quick trip down to the Sea Lion Restaurant for a wine-y fish dinner.

But what was happening? Why wasn't I getting ready? The sun was about to set. It would be a perfect time to sit at a window table looking over the rocky beach.

Still I did not go. Instead, I opened the sliding glass doors of my room and went out onto the motel deck just feet away from the ocean. I sat down in one of the Casa Malibu's bent-bamboo chairs and put my feet up on the weathered, two-by-four railing.

Gently, gently a voice began speaking inside of me. I thought I recognized it as the still voice of the Lord. He was saying, "What area do you think your problem with alcohol is in? Is it physical?"

Physical? I could certainly feel the desire pulling at me right there, sitting on the porch. Yes, that was it, I had a physical addiction.

"Are you sure?"

Well, maybe there was more to it.

"How about your work…is this a work problem?"

It was certainly that. Remember that interview last month when I asked questions through a morning-after haze? Yes, this was a work problem.

"Are you sure?"

Thoroughly bewildered, I waited but heard nothing more. So I got up, stepped back through the glass doors and found my Bible. There was only one temptation area left. I re-read how Satan challenged Jesus to throw Himself from a pinnacle of the temple; He would be safe because He had special divine protection. Jesus answered, "It is said, 'You shall not tempt the Lord your God'" (Luke 4:12 RSV).

I did not see the parallel. What did the temptation to jump from a pinnacle have to do with drinking? I could not reach a conclusion that night, but neither did I go to the Sea Lion.

I did go the next evening, however, with my writer friend Bob Owen. We sat now at the very window booth which I had intended to occupy last evening, with waves crashing on the rocks below. A waitress wearing white space shoes bent over us.

"What will you have to drink?"

Bob said, "Nothing thanks," and I found myself saying I didn't want anything either. So the waitress put two outsized menus down before us and padded off. As soon as she was gone I spoke to Bob about my puzzlement.

"I've been trying to stop drinking, Bob. With very little success I might say. I keep falling back. Part of my problem is that wine is so Biblical."

Bob leaned back on the plastic seat and once again I had the experience of hearing the clarion voice of God in the casual remark of a friend. I'm sure Bob did not know he was speaking for God, but that's typical of this kind of prophecy. He said quietly, "I understand. You're abusing your Scriptural privilege."

The words crashed through my mind. Bob turned his attention to the tabloid-sized menu, but my mind clutched at what he had just said. Abuse of Scriptural privilege! Of course. That's why this was a *spiritual* problem. That's why the Lord had led me last night to the third of Jesus' temptations, where Satan threw a spiritual decision at Jesus. He reminded Jesus, quite accurately, that He had a privileged position. Angels would care for Him so completely that He would not even stub His toe. He *could* in fact appear on the pinnacle of the temple, as ancient tradition foretold the Christ would do, then demonstrate His Messiahship by a spectacular leap, walking away unscathed before the adoring throng. But Jesus knew that this wasn't at all the Father's route for Him. Jesus had a far harder, more agonizing road to follow. To duck the agony would not please the Father. And, as always, Jesus chose the route that left Him in the Father's company.

The waitress was back again, pencil poised. Bob ordered while I made a quick, finger-stabbing decision from the menu. We went on to talk about other things and never did get back to the subject so much on my mind.

Later that evening, sitting again in the moonlight on the raw-wood deck of the motel, I compared my temptation with Jesus'. I had the full Scriptural privilege of drinking wine. But in my case, to use that privilege would be to abuse it. I had taken wine past the point of joy, health and gladness of heart. To expect God to protect me, keep me safe physically, emotionally and spiritually while continuing to abuse wine would be to deliberately challenge Him.

That night I got around at last to doing what Jesus did. He used a verse of Scripture against Satan's temptation, and I would do the same. I asked the Father to give me the defensive tool that I could use forever in my problem temptation.

And He did, by bringing to mind a verse I had heard all my life. That is, I *thought* I had heard it. The portion I knew said, "Resist the devil, and he will flee from you" (James 4:7 NIV).

But for some reason I had never seen this quotation in its entirety. For when I went inside and looked up the reference I found that the complete verse is, "Submit yourselves, then, to God. Resist the devil, and he will flee from you." That's not two verses, it's one. One thought: Submit first, then you can resist.

I must strike an attitude of submittedness to the Lord on this issue of alcohol. It would have to be a permanent way of life. I had goofed. I had abused a Scriptural privilege. The result was a near disaster. My job was no longer to try to change myself, but to put abstinence in His keeping. Then in an attitude of yieldedness I could resist Satan by availing myself of *God's* power as it flowed dynamically through my Arsenal Verse.

I have not had a drink since that day. Satan has tried to undermine my freedom by hurling counterfeit motive verses at me. When Satan tires of this, he whispers that my new approach is no different from other forever decisions. But Satan is lying. This time *is* different because I am no longer depending on myself. I am free because God makes me free, not because I am strong or have risen above my problem.

I still need, quite regularly, to call on my Power Verse. But every time I do, the results are the same: the temptation itself disappears and I move one small step closer to God.

13

The Unfolding Master Plan

I had begun to see, over the past months, that Jesus in the wilderness was revealing a Master Plan for handling problems.

I

Before the Battle

The first step in that plan required me to do some work before problems emerged. I should have certain tools and attitudes at the ready.

1) I would have Arsenal Verses stored and ready to use on the instant.

2) I would not be dismayed at the presence of problems in my life, remembering that the Spirit Himself led Jesus, and He also leads me, into the wilderness.

3) I will be confident that I can distinguish Satan's voice from God's in the upcoming problems. Satan will try to lead me away from my desire to focus on God. I can identify Satan's presence by the Holy Spirit's gift of the Discerning of Spirits (1 Corinthians 12:10). My discernment will be confirmed if I observe some distinctive satanic traits. The devil will always try to leave me:

- with my eyes turned toward the problem rather than toward God
- grasping at thoughts that will prove my own "superiority"
- feeling judgmental and self-righteous
- stirred up, angry
- unyielded, with myself in control
- abusing privileges of power or freedom
- trying to go around a problem, not through it.

II

In the heat of Battle

During the encounter itself I will both swiftly and with simplicity put into practice the Three Only's of Jesus:

1) There is *only one problem*, which is to stay in God's presence.
2) There is *only one hope*. If I want to face my problem the way Jesus did I can hope in God's strength alone, not in my own cleverness, or in any other ally.
3) There is *only one weapon* which I can draw upon if I follow Jesus' example, and that is the correct use of Power Verses which the Father highlights on a page of Scripture or brings to my mind from my arsenal of verses that I have memorized.

I can be confident that I have heard God's choice of Scripture because God's verse for me for this situation leaves me:

- looking toward Him and not toward the problem
- finding Him in the midst of the problem
- filled with a confidence that has absolutely nothing to do with the externals of the situation
- waiting expectantly to see what He will do
- at peace, even in these most difficult circumstances.

III

After the Battle

After countering Satan's temptations I will watch to see how God will put me to work.

How well I remember the day I first began to suspect that there was an "after" stage in the Master Plan. The possibility began to emerge immediately following my first trip without alcohol.

"Lord, I can't handle this alone," I reminded myself on the morning of the flight. "It's not my strength but Your word that will be effective today." I repeated aloud the James 4:7 verse which God had given me for battle, "Submit yourselves then to God. Resist the devil and he will flee from you."

At the airport there was the usual wait between check-in and boarding the plane for Charlotte. But with the help of this verse I spent my time not having wine at the bar, but working on my speech.

The verse was alive in my mind when the stewardess came by a few minutes after take-off for drink orders. "I'll have a Bloody Mary mix, please. Just the mix."

She smiled at me. "We call that a Bloody Shame," she said.

Later there was the lonely evening in the hotel. Here too, I ate my dinner and went up to the room without so much as a glass of California chablis.

That was what I remembered about the trip to Charlotte. With the help of the power inherent in a verse of Scripture, spoken into a situation, an old temptation had been successfully withstood.

But apparently something else also took place on that trip. I remember meeting Martin after the conference. I recall that he was in his mid-fifties, lean to the point of gauntness and wore his hair in a then-unstylish crew cut. Martin had just seen his family business go into receivership and he needed someone—not from the Charlotte area—to talk to.

For an hour we sat on a stone bench in the garden of the conference center and just visited. While Martin told me about his feelings I prayed silently. Then I made one or two observations. That was it.

And yet, after I returned to New York, Martin wrote not just once, but three times, to say how much that hour in the garden meant to him. Those minutes, he said, had changed his life.

How could that possibly be!

I had not felt that my comments were especially wise or penetrating. Obviously, the Holy Spirit had used me as a vehicle to reach Martin. Could it be that I had been usable in this case because, for once, I had encountered a problem in my own life *without* stepping outside of the Spirit?

Several weeks later, still another verse of Scripture helped me win a battle against an ailment common to so many men and women—the sexual fantasy. Much contemporary literature does not consider this a problem at all, but a pleasant escape from loneliness or frustration or rejection. With me it began early in my marriage as a mild form of escapism, tied to loneliness—or more to the point, aloneness.

It didn't matter whether Tib went away from me, or I from her; it didn't matter whether we were apart for business or family reasons. My response was usually the same: my thought patterns went on a binge.

For a while it was all in my mind. Then the time came when I began to drift over to magazine stands and thumb through pornographic literature. As time passed, I started to buy these magazines. Then if I were lonesome in a distant city some strange sense told me where the X-rated movies were. This never happened except when I was separated from Tib.

I reacted to this pattern in two ways. I could imagine one set of friends saying, "I don't understand your worry. You're too goody-goody. What are you, some kind of monk?" Or I could imagine another set of friends saying, "You are a Christian now and supposedly born again to new and victorious life. When are you going to grow up?"

The trouble was that after listening to these two imaginary conversations, which doubtless reflected two sides of my own personality, I knew without doubt which was the real me. Those secret adventures were a most serious matter for *me* for two reasons. There was always the possibility that thoughts would become deeds; this was Satan's goal. Secondly, exposure to sex material always got directly in the way of my ability to focus on God.

So it was clear to me that I should change. And that's precisely where the trouble came, because try as I might, my will power did not help me. I always went right ahead with the same old reaction every time Tib and I were separated; and later I always reacted to these escapes in the same way too, determining to mend my ways. But when next time rolled around I went through the same response.

I took the issue to a psychiatrist friend. He had a name for it. "We call your compulsion a 'separation anxiety syndrome,'" the doctor said. "If it's any comfort, and it probably isn't, you've got lots of company."

The doctor was right. It wasn't much comfort thinking of the large number of people who fought this same battle. Several weeks later as Tib was getting ready for a trip, I became numb with anxiety. When she was gone, if I followed my usual pattern, I knew exactly what I would do.

Still...

Then the thought came—have you tried the Bible? I had not been dynamic in putting the Bible to work against this compulsion. The pattern was too old. What if it failed! Besides, the Bible would probably try to correct me and I already *knew* how I should be acting.

But now, as Tib went up to pack, I remembered that I hadn't even tried to read my Bible that morning. We still had an hour before time to leave for the airport. So reluctantly I went down to my office, found the appointed selection and read Joshua's challenge to the people of Israel, who were being tempted to follow other gods. My pulse quickened. I really didn't want to hear another sermon.

Then, all of a sudden, there it was. The now-familiar experience of a verse standing out from the page. But this time there was something different. It was as if God knew perfectly well that I needed a new approach to my difficulty. If I had been so thoroughly conditioned by defeat that I was beaten before I even started, something different was needed. And He gave it to me. For these were the nine words that illuminated themselves on the page, "...choose for yourselves this day whom you will serve..." (Joshua 24:15).

I put the Bible down, for I knew I was at a watershed.

Make up your mind *now,* Joshua was saying to the people, whom you will serve. Here was a guideline for recurring and predictable problems. I shouldn't try to do battle at the *point* of temptation. With my old record, I had preconditioned myself to fail. But suppose I reversed that and preconditioned myself to success by fighting the battle *now,* ahead of time, while I was still on solid ground, before I got into the quagmire.

"Lord, I do just what Joshua did," I said aloud, standing there in my office. "Not later, but now, *this day,* I choose to serve You and not feed this lustful interest."

Tib left. And sure enough, as predictable as a tide this compulsion rolled in. The drive engulfed me: come on, slip out to the nearest dealer. In the past my will power had not saved me from the irresistible undertow.

But not now. I just didn't yield.

Not because I had suddenly become stronger, but because I had set my course ahead of time. The application of my Power Verse occurred hours ago, not at the point of temptation. And that made all the difference.

The remarkable thing was that although I was still faced with the old compulsion, I was never really tempted. Every time the alluring ideas flicked at my emotions I reminded myself of the word from Joshua and discovered that the battle had already been won.

To this day whenever I face separation, I prepare ahead of time with God's Power Verse, confident that He will then fight my battle for me.

Perhaps this is what Jesus had in mind when He taught His disciples the model defensive prayer, "Lead us not into temptation, but deliver us from the evil one." Perhaps He meant that we should try to avoid confronting Satan at the point of our greatest weakness, but that we could ask the Father to provide our delivery ahead of time. Then when the struggle comes, victory is already there...

Well, it happened that just after this first triumphant experience with an old temptation, a woman telephoned who was facing a crisis in her home. Her teen-age daughter had run away with a married man, and now wanted to come back home. The woman's husband threatened to throw the girl out bodily if she dared "so much as to open my door." Again, just as I had done with Martin a few weeks earlier, we talked, but I cannot remember saying anything that sounded to me like wisdom; although it is true that an odd boldness swept over me as we talked and prayed together. When I asked God to come to the rescue of this family I sensed His closeness.

Our phone visit was over. In due course Tib came back home. Then one night the phone rang again. It was the woman with the crisis at home.

"You'd probably like to know," she said, "how our prayers were answered. Things are not only all right at home, they're better than they've ever been."

What was going on!

As I reviewed these two recent experiences, it was clear to me that some uncustomary force was flowing through me; a formidable intercessory energy that went way beyond my own ability to help. Surely it was related to successful handling of problem-temptations. If Satan treats problems as red herrings, trying to get us to focus on our trials rather than on God, and if we say No to that temptation, then maybe afterwards we are always given a job to do.

Did this happen to Jesus?

I opened my Bible to see. I knew that He had gone into His temptation in the Spirit, and that He came out of the wilderness still in the Spirit, but it came as a surprise to me that this experience was *immediately* followed by the beginning of Jesus' ministry to people in need. He spelled out exactly what He would be doing:

> *The Spirit of the Lord is upon me, because he hath anointed me to preach the gospel to the poor; he hath sent me to heal the brokenhearted, to preach deliverance to the captives, and recovering of sight to the blind, to set at liberty them that are bruised.*

> Luke 4:18 KJV

There it was, all in one chapter. I turned to Matthew and Mark and they told the same story, making a direct linkage between being led into problems by God, taking an active step in the middle of the problem *toward* God, and then being put to work *for* God.

The pattern was too clear to miss. Handled correctly, all our problems are going somewhere! They then immediately lead into work for others. We will be given a job to do. It is special work, prepared for us by the Lord ahead of time. "For we are his workmanship, created in Christ Jesus for good works, which God prepared beforehand, that we should walk in them" (Ephesians 2:10 RSV).

And often these good works which God has prepared for us are full of surprises and adventure which we could never plan for or anticipate.

14

The Best of All for Last

I have to admit that I was dragging my feet on our way to Tarrytown, New York; a twenty-minute drive from our home. It was a Friday evening, just coming on six o'clock, and I'd much rather be heading out for dinner with Tib than toward Marymount, a mammoth, red-brick pile covering acres of real estate on a hilltop near the Hudson River. I knew that Marymount had been a fine girls' school, but that like so many once-prospering religious institutions in the Hudson Valley, it had fallen on hard times. A handful of nuns tried to stay together by using the buildings in whatever way came to hand—as a day-care center, as a facility rented out for business conferences and, as in our case, as a meeting place for retreat groups. The weekend to which we were headed was called by the puzzling and more than a little frightening name, "Marriage Encounter."

Friends had gone on a weekend retreat here. They came back enthusiastic, stating flatly that Marriage Encounter would change our lives—which promise was oddly threatening, and perhaps accounted for my present feet-dragging.

But, here we were, turning through the gate into the grounds of Marymount.

They put us in a tiny third floor room which overlooked a stand, down near the driveway, where a smiling nun was trying to raise a few dollars by selling potted plants to visitors. I don't know why that glimpse of dogged bravery put me in a more receptive mind, but it did: by the time we were seated in a semicircle in the main conference room downstairs, I was feeling less defensive. There were thirty-one couples in the room, three of whom had been on this weekend before and were active as our leaders along with a priest. The priest intrigued me. When his turn came to introduce himself, John Mihelko told us in a voice so low it was hard to follow his words, that until his order had been kicked out he had been a missionary to China. An introspective man with deep-set, shadow-rimmed eyes, John Mihelko now pastored a church in lower Manhattan's Chinatown.

Was everyone else as nervous as I was? The leaders passed out notebooks and ball-point pens that wrote sporadically. We sat in silence, wondering what we were supposed to do.

Two days later, Tib and I stood side by side in our pews in the church-sized chapel of Marymount. Resting on the marble altar at the east end of the sanctuary along with those of the other couples, were the notebooks we had been given last Friday night. We fought back tears of gratitude that we had found each other thirty years before. Gratitude that we had a family that was real, and not just the shell it might have been. Gratitude for the new art we had just learned, symbolized by the notebooks which lay on the altar.

Led by John Mihelko we now repeated our marriage vows. All around us other couples were doing the same. John renewed his priestly vows too. Then, slowly, as couples, we were called forward to the altar to receive from John's hands the two notebooks which we had placed there earlier. John had a personal blessing for each couple. It was a long process, and I found myself reviewing just what these notebooks contained. A special kind of Love Letter, John had called the messages scribbled on their pages. Over this long and exhausting weekend each husband or wife had written to the other many times, letters of a unique quality, meant for his spouse's eyes only. There was no doubt in my mind that in these epistles, Marriage Encounter had found a tool Tib and I would always be thankful for.

The concept of Marriage Encounter was born in the early sixties in Spain where a young priest, Gabriel Salvo, was working with couples, trying to help them reaffirm the strength of their marriages. Father Salvo noticed that often, whenever there was unhappiness in the home, the partners had stopped listening to each other's *feelings*. They were dealing exclusively with issues—as important as it was to deal with issues—rather than with each other's emotions. Which was too bad, because it is through feelings that we have the most direct experience of another person. What would happen if these couples could be taught to share their hopes and fears again, just as they had when they first fell in love? As soon as he started to work with this idea Father Salvo discovered a secret. Couples who had been married for a while could communicate better on paper than they could by confronting each other in direct dialogue.

This was the origin of Marriage Encounter. Parents by the thousands came into more creative relationship with each other, children no longer had to act out their anxieties. After a presentation of his findings at Notre Dame, an American priest, Father Chuck Gallagher, began to develop the idea here in the United States. Today more than a million men and women have taken part in the Marriage Encounter experience.*

At the heart of Marriage Encounter, then, is the notebook, where each partner writes his Love Letters. We were not to write about issues, but about the emotions which a given issue aroused in us. The key was to avoid judgment, opinion, criticism. Instead we were to center down on one question: "How does that make me feel?"

"Feelings are neither right nor wrong," we were told. "They just are. So write about your emotions without apology." We were assigned starting-point subjects to explore:

---

* For further information write Marriage Encounter, 567 Morris Avenue, Elizabeth, New Jersey 07208.

What do I like best about you? How does that make me feel?
What do I like best about myself? How does that make me feel?
What do I like best about us? How does that make me feel?

For at least ten minutes we were to write, always applying the yardstick, "Is this a judgment, or am I really sharing the way I feel?"

Then came the second step. When we finished writing, we were to exchange notebooks with each other. We were to absorb the contents of each other's letters. "Read the letter twice," the leaders told us. "Once for what is actually said, and a second time for the person peering, however timidly, through the lines."

After we had written our Love Letter, after we had exchanged and read each other's epistles, we were to talk about the feelings expressed. "For no longer than ten minutes," John Mihelko said. "That's about as long as most people can stick to feelings without getting bogged down in problems and solutions."

So we separated from the group to experiment with our "ten and ten" as Marriage Encounter calls these pairs of write-and-dialogue sessions. We were astonished to discover that there were dozens of feelings we had never explored. Once the first dialogue was completed we returned to the conference room for our next topic, then for another, and another, and another. That first night we dialogued until three in the morning.

We were exhausted, of course. After breakfast the next morning, when we were back in our room ready to face dialogue topic number five, we began to fight. Tib complained that I was not following directions; I complained that she was not listening to what I had to *say*. Then we had an idea. Why not let this very fight be the subject of our next letter to each other?

It turned out, when we joined the semicircle downstairs, that other couples had been fighting too. In fact, we were all going through a marriage in microcosm. After a honeymoon of superb communication came a period of very low communication, bickering and despair. This, the leaders pointed out, was an expected part of every healthy marriage. Other couples had also handled their negative feelings by a "ten and ten," on the spot, and they too not only passed through the disagreement unscathed but had come out on the other side closer than ever to each other.

And now in the chapel at Marymount, John Mihelko was calling our names. Tib and I held hands like a couple of teenagers as we stepped out into the aisle and walked forward to the altar. John's deepset eyes were alive with joy as he placed his hands on our two notebooks and asked the Lord to bless them and urged us to continue our ten-and-ten daily, letting the circumstances of the hour suggest the dialogue.

"You know," John Mihelko said, looking up and speaking to the entire group in that whisper-low voice of his, "…you know…" he said again, and then John touched on the idea which was to round out my entire adventure with Scripture, "…it has always seemed to me that the Bible is God's Love Letter to us. We should read His Letter the way we do our own, twice: once for what is being said and a second time for the Person showing forth between the lines."

⚊ ⚊ ⚊ ⚊

The weekend was over. We were fatigued, but we were also certain that we had made a good retreat. Not only because of the new tool we had in our marriage, but because of the whole new way of approaching the Bible that had been suggested at the last moment at the altar.

That same night during my quiet time I found myself looking at the Bible with fresh eyes, thinking about the enormity of the task God has in making Himself known to people. In reaching toward us, perhaps He always takes us through a pattern similar to the one I had experienced. At first, I raced through the Bible, absorbing the joy of shared love. Then, God began to show me that He wanted to be a part of the struggles I was facing: how do you discipline a child, handle an addiction, resolve competitiveness?

Important as these areas were, as revealing as they were of His caring, there was a still more profound way of reading the Bible. I should offer my feelings to Him and I should try to catch something of *His* feelings too. I should be alert for the Person who was trying, through the medium of human language, somehow to convey the vastness of an unutterable love.

So that night I tried something new to me. I came to the Bible with nothing particular in mind, just letting Him talk to me about our lives together, telling me how He feels about any given situation at hand.

I started to read the Psalm appointed for that evening.

> *Bless the Lord, O my soul: and all that is within me, bless his holy name.*
> *Bless the Lord, O my soul, and forget not all his benefits:*
> *Psalm 103:1-2* KJV

Then I imagined what it would be like for God to hear these words being said by His people. "That's good. That's how I want you to feel," He might be saying. "You're beginning to glimpse a fraction of My total, self-giving nature."

I read the entire Psalm with this listening ear, trying to feel things with God. To my mind came other words of His, spoken to Moses on Mt. Sinai. "…for I the Lord thy God am a jealous God…" (Exodus 20:5 KJV). Jealous, not in a negative, clutching, suspicious way, but jealous as a positive, creative fact. God is jealous because He cares enough for us to want the unique best for us: Himself alone. Our highest goal is to reach toward one prize only, God Himself. We fall short if ever we:

use God: I want God at my side so that *I* can achieve a goal…

divide God: I love Him and want to serve Him; but to be practical…

doubt God: I trust God, of course, but…

Whenever we do fall for one of these temptations we dilute the richness of the prize, which is closeness to God. God alone is the measure of success in problem handling. That is where we are headed.

And what is the role of the Bible in pressing toward this mark? I could see it at last. We were at our best when we read the Bible for companionship with God.

God wanted us to use Scripture in the way Jesus did. He wanted us to store up His word, which He would infuse with power in present situations. He wanted us to speak forth His word, sending it into our problems.

But always, He yearned for us to use that Scripture toward the highest goal of all—the enjoyment of Himself for Himself alone.

Appendix One: My Arsenal

*T*hese are some of the Bible passages which *I* memorized. Each individual's arsenal of Scripture will be different, of course, fitted to his own welfare.

My particular choices do not even attempt to provide a balanced survey of Biblical resources; on the contrary, each one was chosen to meet a specific need and reflects my rather one-track preoccupation at the time.

Unless otherwise noted, all quotations are from the New International Version.

When I'm immobilized by worry:

1. Do not be anxious about anything, but in everything, by prayer and petition, with thanksgiving, present your requests to God. And the peace of God, which transcends all understanding, will guard your hearts and your minds in Christ Jesus (Philippians 4:6,7).

Or by guilt:

2. Therefore, there is now no condemnation for those who are in Christ Jesus (Romans 8:1).

My alcohol Power Verse:

3. Submit yourselves, then, to God. Resist the devil, and he will flee from you (James 4:7).

My Power Verse for work:

4. And lead us not into temptation, but deliver us from the evil one (Matthew 6:13).

The Bible as guide:

5. Your word is a lamp to my feet and a light for my path (Psalm 119:105).

The Bible as protection:

6. Direct my footsteps according to your word; let no sin rule over me (Psalm 119:133).

7. I have hidden your word in my heart that I might not sin against you (Psalm 119:11).

The Bible as the way to:

8. Look to the Lord and his strength; seek his face always (Psalm 105:4).

When facing temptation:

9. When the devil had finished all this tempting, he left him until an opportune time. Jesus returned to Galilee in the power of the Spirit... (Luke 4:13,14).

10. For whatever is hidden is meant to be disclosed, and whatever is concealed is meant to be brought out into the open (Mark 4:22).

11. You have set our iniquities before you, our secret sins in the light of your presence (Psalm 90:8).

Where temptations come from:

12. Put on the full armor of God so that you can take your stand against the devil's schemes. For our struggle is not against flesh and blood, but against the rulers, against the authorities, against the powers of this dark world and against the spiritual forces of evil in the heavenly realms (Ephesians 6:11,12).

13. Stand firm then, with the belt of truth buckled around your waist, with the breastplate of righteousness in place, and with your feet fitted with the readiness that comes from the gospel of peace. In addition to all this, take up the shield of faith, with which you can extinguish all the flaming arrows of the evil one. Take the helmet of salvation and the sword of the Spirit, which is the word of God (Ephesians 6:14-17).

14. Finally, brothers, whatever is true, whatever is noble, whatever is right, whatever is pure, whatever is lovely, whatever is admirable—if anything is excellent or praiseworthy—think about such things (Philippians 4:8).

I'm apprehensive:

15. So do not fear, for I am with you; do not be dismayed, for I am your God. I will strengthen you and help you; I will uphold you with my righteous right hand (Isaiah 41:10).

My work was planned ahead of time:

16. For we are God's workmanship, created in Christ Jesus to do good works, which God prepared in advance for us to do (Ephesians 2:10).

Controlling physical appetites:

17. Dear friends, I urge you, as aliens and strangers in the world, to abstain from sinful desires, which war against your soul (1 Peter 2:11).

Grace when dieting:

18. Who satisfies your desires with good things so that your youth is renewed like the eagle's (Psalm 103:5).

Lines from His Love Letter:

19. The friendship of the Lord is for those who fear him, and he makes known to them his covenant (Psalm 25:14 RSV).

20. ...he will rejoice over you with singing (Zephaniah 3:17).

My reply:

21. Praise the Lord, O my soul; all my inmost being, praise his holy name (Psalm 103:1).

22. Because your love is better than life, my lips will glorify you (Psalm 63:3).

On opening the Bible:

23. For the word of God is living and active. Sharper than any double-edged sword, it penetrates even to dividing soul and spirit, joints and marrow; it judges the thoughts and attitudes of the heart (Hebrews 4:12).

On closing the Bible:

24. I rejoice in your promise like one who finds great spoil (Psalm 119:162).

When I'm tired:

25. ...In repentance and rest is your salvation, in quietness and trust is your strength... (Isaiah 30:15).

26. He gives strength to the weary and increases the power of the weak (Isaiah 40:29).

27. Let us not become weary in doing good, for at the proper time we will reap a harvest if we do not give up (Galatians 6:9).

For a dry spell:

28. O God, you are my God, earnestly I seek you; my soul thirsts for you, my body longs for you, in a dry and weary land where there is no water. I have seen you in the sanctuary and beheld your power and your glory (Psalm 63:1,2).

When I am wrongly criticized:

29. Rulers persecute me without cause, but my heart trembles at your word (Psalm 119:161).

30. But how is it to your credit if you receive a beating for doing wrong and endure it? But if you suffer for doing good and you endure it, this is commendable before God (1 Peter 2:20).

31. [Speaking of Jesus] When they hurled their insults at him, he did not retaliate; when he suffered, he made no threats. Instead, he entrusted himself to him who judges justly (1 Peter 2:23).

When I am rightly criticized:

32. Praise the Lord, O my soul, and forget not all his benefits—who forgives all your sins and heals all your diseases, who redeems your life from the pit and crowns you with love and compassion (Psalm 103:2-4).

33. He does not treat us as our sins deserve or repay us according to our iniquities. For as high as the heavens are above the earth, so great is his love for those who fear him; as far as the east is from the west, so far has he removed our transgressions from us (Psalm 103:10-12).

34. As a father has compassion on his children, so the Lord has compassion on those who fear him; for he knows how we are formed, he remembers that we are dust (Psalm 103:13,14).

When I face something I'm afraid of:

35. For you did not receive the spirit of slavery to fall back into fear, but you have received the spirit of sonship (Romans 8:15 RSV).

Moment-by-moment inspiration:

36. Whenever you are arrested and brought to trial, do not worry beforehand about what to say. Just say whatever is given you at the time, for it is not you speaking, but the Holy Spirit (Mark 13:11).

Loving my fellow Christians:

37. Then Peter began to speak: "I now realize how true it is that God does not show favoritism but accepts men from every nation who fear him and do what is right (Acts 10:34,35).

When my heart can't contain my love for Him:

38. Praise the Lord, you his angels, you mighty ones who do his bidding, who obey his word. Praise the Lord, all his heavenly hosts, you his servants who do his will. Praise the Lord, all his works everywhere in his dominion (Psalm 103:20-22).

When I'm depressed:

39. Why are you downcast, O my soul? Why so disturbed within me? Put your hope in God, for I will yet praise him, my Savior and my God (Psalm 42:11).

When things seem to go wrong:

40. The Lord has established his throne in heaven, and his kingdom rules over all (Psalm 103:19).
41. I know that thou canst do all things, and that no purpose of thine can be thwarted (Job 42:2 RSV).

When I must handle the business side of ministry:

42. Do not store up for yourselves treasures on earth, where moth and rust destroy, and where thieves break in and steal. But store up for yourselves treasures in heaven, where moth and rust do not destroy, and where thieves do not break in and steal. For where your treasure is, there your heart will be also (Matthew 6:19-21).
43. Though your riches increase, do not set your heart on them (Psalm 62:10).

Once God has given me the victory:

44. If we deliberately keep on sinning after we have received the knowledge of the truth, no sacrifice for sins is left, but only a fearful expectation of judgment and of raging fire that will consume the enemies of God (Hebrews 10:26,27).
45. In spite of all this, they kept on sinning; in spite of his wonders, they did not believe. So he ended their days in futility and their years in terror (Psalm 78:32,33).

Sticking with it:

46. And pray in the Spirit on all occasions with all kinds of prayers and requests. With this in mind, be alert and always keep on praying for all the saints (Ephesians 6:18).

Promises, when I stick with it:

47. He is like a tree planted by steams of water, which yields its fruit in season and whose leaf does not wither. Whatever he does prospers (Psalms 1:3).

48. [He has given us] an inheritance that can never perish, spoil or fade—kept in heaven for you (1 Peter 1:4).

49. The mind of sinful man is death, but the mind controlled by the Spirit is life and peace (Romans 8:6).

When I begin to think this uphill Christian walk was my own idea:

50. For he chose us in him before the creation of the world to be holy and blameless in his sight (Ephesians 1:4).

One reason for suffering:

51. Who comforts us in all our troubles, so that we can comfort those in any trouble with the comfort we ourselves have received from God (2 Corinthians 1:4).

Another reason:

52. No discipline seems pleasant at the time, but painful. Later on, however, it produces a harvest of righteousness and peace for those who have been trained by it (Hebrews 12:11).

53. The fear of the Lord is the beginning of knowledge, and fools despise wisdom and discipline (Proverbs 1:7).

54. I consider that our present sufferings are not worth comparing with the glory that will be revealed in us (Romans 8:18).

Appendix Two:
Bible Reading Programs

1. Lectionaries:

a) Episcopalian—*The Church Lesson Calendar*. Morehouse-Barlow Co., 78 Danbury Road, Wilton, Conn. 06897.

b) Lutheran—*The New Lectionary*. Fortress Press, 2900 Queen Lane, Philadelphia, Pa. 19129.

c) Presbyterian—*The Worship Book*. The Westminster Press, 902 Witherspoon Bldg., Philadelphia, Pa. 19107.

d) Roman Catholic—*The Ordo*. The Paulist Press, 545 Island Road, Rumsey, N.J. 07446.

2. The Moravian Daily Texts

The Moravian Board of Education, 5 Market Street, Bethlehem, Pa. 18018.

Peter Marshall's favorite. One of the first daily devotional books. Came out originally in 1731, and has been published continuously ever since.

3. Scripture Union

1716 Spruce St., Philadelphia, Pa. 19103

a) *Daily Bread*—An in-depth Bible study. Goes through the Bible in four years. Interpretive comment on Scripture passages as an aid for daily Bible reading and prayer.

b) *Discovery*—Moves consecutively through Bible, covering 10-15 verses a day. Takes reader through the New Testament twice and most of Old Testament once every four years.

c) *Bible Study Book*—Designed to cover the whole Bible along with Commentary. Program completed in five years.

d) *Bible Characters and Doctrines*—Sections presenting both characters and doctrines in each book providing balance and variety in the selected subjects. Four years to complete.

4. Daily Light

Samuel Bagster and Sons Ltd., 72 Marylebone Lane, London WI, England

A selection of verses for every morning and evening. A classic devotional text using words of Scripture.

5. Search the Scriptures

Inter-Varsity Press, Downers Grove, Ill. 60515

Three year program of study, provides variety. Similar to Inter-Varsity's *Search the Scriptures* is John Baillie's *Diary of Private Reading*, Charles Scribner's Sons, N.Y., N.Y.

6. My Utmost for Highest

Dodd, Mead & Company, 79 Madison Ave., N.Y., N.Y.

By Oswald Chambers. Selections for every day of the year—for the Christian who is eager to be challenged by unusual insights.

7. Daily Walk

The Navigators, P. O. Box 20, Colorado Springs, Colo. 80901

A Scripture reading and comment on given passages. Covers entire Bible.

8. The One-Year Bible

Tyndale House Publishers, 336 Gundersen Drive, Wheaton, Ill. 60189

The text of the entire Living Bible divided into the 365 days of the year. Every day you read a passage from the Old Testament and one from the New Testament along with a psalm and a proverb or two. (Also available in other versions.)

9. Personal Prayer Diary

YWAM Publishers, P.O. Box 55787, Seattle, Wash. 98155

A diary with space to write daily entries concerning your times with the Lord. A daily Bible reading guide is given so that in the course of a year you will read the Old Testament once and the New Testament, Psalms and Proverbs twice. You are also given unreached people groups to pray for daily.

Appendix Three:
Questions on Each Chapter

Chapter One

Why was the author's spiritual life ebbing? Give a key reason.

Once the above problem was identified, what did the author set out to do?

Chapter Two

What important lessons did the author learn in Chapter Two?

Chapter Three

Why was the author conditioned to react negatively to the subject of Biblical literalness?

What should we do to overcome this trap in "inherited emotions"?

What happened in John Sherrill's life that helped him see that the Bible is to be taken more literally than his father had taught him?

Chapter Four

What does it mean when a verse of Scripture "burns within you" or "leaps from the page"?

Has this ever happened to you? If so, describe an incident.

What gave John Sherrill a new reason and excitement for the Scriptures?

Verses leaping from the page could relate to a variety of situations, but they all have one thing in common. What?

Why did these "leaping from the page" verses stop occurring for a while in the author's life? Give a Scripture that supports the principle involved.

Chapter Five

Why is it significant that God highlighted a verse for John *before* the royalty check arrived—aside from helping him through the temptation?

Explain the difference between a Manna verse and an Arsenal one.

Chapter Six

Give the key to memorization that the author found. Name two other keys.

With Arsenal verses, why is it possible to memorize just a portion of a long verse and yet it will be effective?

If you have an area of weakness in your life, what kind of verses should you learn?

Chapter Seven

In the framework of the concept of "having [an Arsenal Verse] (by itself)...isn't enough," comment on the phrase, "...if God did everything automatically, He would be violating my free will." What is the author meaning here?

Chapter Eight

In your own words, what is the lesson for us to learn in this chapter?

Chapter Nine

Until now the author has been spoken to by the Lord through the Bible concerning such problems as a dog, a real estate cheat and an under-age son driving a car. What problems are we looking at in this chapter?

Explain: Could I learn to treat all problems the way Jesus did? "Could I learn to treat all problems as the single temptation to move out from the Spirit?"

Chapter Ten

Jesus could have used a miracle, an angel or even prayer to handle the temptation that came to Him when He was hungry—but He used what? If that's what the Son of God resorted to, what should we do?

Chapter Eleven

Explain the steps the author took to overcome his fear of a reoccurrence of cancer and its pain.

What are some of the red herring problems that demand our attention and take us from what should be the real focus of our lives (mentioned after the author's testimony about his time on Nantucket Island)?

What are some other red herring problems that you can think of?

After the author's discovery of himself (through the key-lost-in-the-compactor episode) what Power Verse did he use, and when did he use it?

Chapter Twelve

What "Power Verse" did the author use to help him with his drinking habit? What has been the result?

Chapter Thirteen

What was the result spiritually when the author became exposed to sex material?

In his battle with lust (by using a Power Verse), what made all the difference?

In his experience with Martin, and then with the lady with the problem at home, what happened in John Sherrill's life *before* each experience that was common to both and made the "counseling" times successful?

Chapter Fourteen

We are at our best when we read the Bible for_____?

God always yearns for us to use Scripture towards the highest goal of all, which is what?

Study Guide

Chapter One

For Self-Examination

What was my attitude toward the Bible after I first came to know Christ?

What is my attitude now?

If my attitude is different now, why has it changed?

How has the Bible provided answers to my problems?

What have I done to make the Bible a personal book for my life?

For Group Discussion

Why do some Christians—individually or as a group—seem to place minimal value on the Bible?

Is carrying a Bible to church necessarily a sign of spiritual maturity? Why or why not?

If the Bible is a "new" book to someone, what are some ways to help that person become more familiar with its format and organization?

How can we as a body of Christians help each other to be more involved with the Bible?

Why is daily time in the Bible crucial to spiritual life?

How can an ancient book, written over thousands of years, offer answers to contemporary, personal problems?

Have group members tell about significant experiences they have had with the Bible.

Have group members talk about how their attitudes toward the
Bible have changed over the years.

ChapterTwo

For Self-Examination

What efforts have I given to "scholarly" study of the Bible?

If I have pursued such study, how have I benefited?

Do I have appropriate tools for such study?

What has been my motivation(s) for scholarly study?

What is my method for regular interaction with the Bible?

How was this method acquired?

Am I satisfied with this method?

If I don't use any set method (or am unsatisfied with the one I use), what should I do to design a program that works for me?

What would be a workable way to set up a Bible reading "accountability system" with another believer?

For Group Discussion
What are the benefits of scholarship, or thorough Biblical study?

What are the risks of over-emphasizing Biblical scholarship?

What are the risks of under-emphasizing Biblical scholarship?

How can we approach Scripture to build up the spirit rather than just the mind?

How can accountability to another Christian ensure success in regular Bible reading?

Brainstorm and discuss the merits and weaknesses of various Bible reading methods.

Have group members tell about methods they have used successfully, or otherwise.

Chapter 3

For Self-Examination

How have other people shaped my former and present attitudes toward the Bible?

How do I now view issues such as the Bible's inspiration, authority, and literalness?

What measures have I taken to analyze and challenge my preconceived notions about the Bible?

What am I saying or doing to affect the way other people view the Bible?

How can I go about identifying and defusing my preconceived ideas and emotions about the Bible?

For Group Discussion

What are some of the preconceived notions that people bring to the
Bible?

What kinds of attitudes toward the Bible might we acquire from the
people who have influenced our lives?

What have well-meaning, conservative Christians sometimes done
to give people a negative view of the Bible's authority and
credibility?

How can we help one another recognize inaccurate preconceived
notions about the Bible?

What are the dangers of an idolatrous attitude toward the Bible?

Chapter 4

For Self-Examination

In what circumstance(s) in my life have I assumed the Bible would
not speak relevantly?

In what unusual circumstances have I been surprised by the Bible's relevance?

Have I witnessed misapplication of the Scripture to life situations (in my life or someone else's)?

What change could I make in my attitude or Bible reading habits that would make me more open to the Bible's speaking to me?

What situations most easily keep me from recognizing God's highlighted verses? How can I begin to counteract this?

For Group Discussion
What kinds of circumstances might people consider beneath the Bible's dignity, or irrelevant to the Bible?

Why can the Bible speak to even the minor irritations in our lives?

How might Scripture be wrongly applied to life situations?

What is it about the Bible that makes it "active" for our specific problems?

What habits or attitudes might interfere with the Bible's speaking to specific life situations?

Chapter 5

For Self-Examination

Why can a verse that seems "alive" to me one day seem lifeless the next?

For what issues in my life am I desiring God to highlight Scripture?

For what issues in my life do I not want God to highlight Scripture?

How can I begin to build a supply of Arsenal Verses?

What past circumstances in my life might have been handled differently if I had had appropriate Arsenal Verses from which to draw?

For Group Discussion

If God's highlighting of a Manna Verse tends to last only one day, what should be our approach to a personal Bible reading program?

What is the significance of a verse being highlighted for another person's benefit?

How can we best take advantage of the difference between Manna Verses and Arsenal Verses?

In what situations would Arsenal Verses be especially useful?

Chapter 6

For Self-Examination

How many memorized verses do I have at my disposal?

What kind of learning/memorization style do I now use? Am I a visual or oral learner?

What kind of memorization program do I now think will meet my needs most effectively?

For Group Discussion
What is the significance of Arsenal Verses in the Christian's life?

Why should we be conscious of our personal learning styles as we attempt to acquire Arsenal Verses?

Brainstorm a variety of personal memorization methods and programs. Do any of these alternatives seem superior—more "spiritual"—than the others? Why?

Chapter 7

For Self-Examination
How frequently do I actively apply a verse that God brings to my attention during a day's reading?

In what situation have I spoken Scripture to deal with a problem? What was the effect?

What attitudes of other personal issues might be hindering me from making a habit of speaking out with Scripture? How might I deal with such a hinderance?

For Group Discussion
What is the difference between recognizing a highlighted Manna Verse and applying that passage?

Why can speaking out with Scripture be so effective in overcoming a problem?

Why does God want our partnership, rather then simply overcoming our problems for us without our involvement?

Chapter 8

For Self-Examination
Are there any decisions I have made—or seen others make—that would have been different if more care had been given to balancing Scripture?

To avoid an imbalanced view of an issue, how should I approach my reading and study of Scripture?

For Group Discussion
What are some other examples of Scripture passages that seem to balance each other?

Why is it important that a passage of Scripture not be allowed to stand alone without support or balance from other passages?

How might we help one another avoid using Scripture in an imbalanced fashion?

Chapter 9

For Self-Examination

What areas in my life have I sometimes tried to shield from the living light of Scripture?

After reading the account of Jesus' temptation, what principles stand out that could be applied to my life?

What problems in my life are a strong force to lure me away from the Spirit?

What time(s) in my life do I recall as having been lived fully in the Spirit?

What does being in the Spirit mean to me?

What are some of the tougher enemies that I face in my spiritual journey?

For Group Discussion

What issues in our lives do we sometimes hide from exposure to God's Word, and from other believers?

What attitudes or preconceptions might prevent us from seeing answers for our own lives in the temptations of Jesus?

Why does the enemy strive so hard to move us away from the Spirit?

How can we encourage one another in our efforts to stay in the Spirit?

Why does the sense of euphoria that often accompanies a person's conversion seem to last only a brief time?

Chapter 10

For Self-Examination

What are tell-tale signs in my life that reveal if something is preventing Scripture from speaking to me?

What challenge exists in my own life that I should share with someone else, rather than bearing it alone?

What Scripture might I use as a weapon when the enemy attacks me in this matter of the Bible being "silent"?

How can I stay in the Spirit even if a problem seemingly remains unsolved?

For Group Discussion

Why can fear cause us to avoid Scripture?

What factors can make Bible reading seem meaningless or ineffective to us?

What happens to us when we try to keep our problems to ourselves?

Why can a Power Verse be effective against a spiritual challenge?

Why is it that each new problem seems to be a new learning experience, rather than a simple matter of applying lessons previously learned?

Chapter 11

For Self-Examination

What have been some of my difficult problems that God has exposed and given ways to solve?

What have been some of those solutions?

Do the solutions God is offering for any of my problems seem too unpleasant? Why?

How might Satan be trying to distract me from God's solutions?

What should I do in response to the enemy's efforts?

For Group Discussion

As in the case of John's competitiveness, why do some of our deep-rooted weaknesses take so long to be revealed and recognized?

Why would God use something as distasteful as crushed garbage to speak to John?

Part of God's solution for John's problem was to have Elizabeth and John stop writing joint projects. Do you think most of God's solutions for problems are this simple? Why?

In applying this solution to the problem, what new problems might the Sherrills encounter?

Chapter 12

For Self-Examination

Is there anyone close to me who is, as John's friend said, abusing a Scriptural privilege?

How do I know that a behavior is a genuine abuse, rather than an affront to my personal views on the matter?

What issues in my life might be susceptible to such abuse?

How should I proceed in examining those issues so God can speak to me about them?

For Group Discussion

How can Scripture be used to justify behavior that is contrary to godliness?

Besides alcohol, what are other issues that might be susceptible to the abuse of a Scriptural privilege?

Is it possible to view someone's behavior as abuse of a Scriptural privilege, though it actually is not? Why?

How can we avoid such a mistake that may lead to undue criticism of the fellow believer?

Chapter 13

For Self-Examination

When the sense of God's presence has been consistent in my life, what have been the results?

What have been the keys to maintaining that sense of God's presence? What things have broken that sense?

What portions of Scriptures have been effective in maintaining my sense of God's presence?

What has been the effect on other people when God's presence has been real in my life?

What is my stubborn spiritual problem? How can I begin using Scripture to solve that problem?

What area of ministry do I think God would open up to me if that stubborn problem was solved?

For Group Discussion

At the beginning of this chapter, John wrote, "...that Jesus in the wilderness was revealing a Master Plan for handling problems." Do you think this Master Plan that John discovered is just for him, or a universal principle? Explain your answer.

What should be our stance toward a principle that a fellow believer "discovers" in the Bible and applies to his life? Should we try to adapt it to our own lives, or see it as a highly individual issue that may not be easily transferable?

As in John's account of his encounter with Martin in Charlotte, why can our experience of God's presence have a profound effect on other people (even without conscious effort on our part)?

Why is willpower often inadequate for dealing with deep-seated character flaws?

Chapter 14

For Self-Examination

How do I react to the idea of approaching the Bible "with nothing particular in mind"?

How might I apply to my Bible reading John Mihelko's comment that ten minutes is the longest period "most people can stick to feelings without getting bogged down in problems and solutions"?

What have been my opinions about God's emotions in general?

What has been my view about God's emotions toward me?

Am I open to changing my views on God's emotions?

As I read the Bible, how can I always keep in mind the priority of reading the Bible for companionship with God?

For Group Discussion

Why did God choose to reveal Himself in writing, rather than by speaking or appearing to each person?

How can the relationship between a person and God be compared to the relationship between a wife and husband?

Why could reading the Bible with an awareness of God's emotions be beneficial to spiritual growth?

What kinds of motivations or objectives might people bring to their reading of the Bible?

What might be the results of each of those objectives?

What should be the primary objective(s) when reading Scripture?